Oxford Grammar for Schools 3

Rachel Godfrey

Great Clarendon Street, Oxford, OX2 6DP, United Kingdom

Oxford University Press is a department of the University of Oxford.
It furthers the University's objective of excellence in research, scholarship,
and education by publishing worldwide. Oxford is a registered trade
mark of Oxford University Press in the UK and in certain other countries

© Oxford University Press 2013

The moral rights of the author have been asserted

First published in 2013

2017 2016 2015 2014 2013
10 9 8 7 6 5 4 3 2

No unauthorized photocopying

All rights reserved. No part of this publication may be reproduced, stored
in a retrieval system, or transmitted, in any form or by any means, without
the prior permission in writing of Oxford University Press, or as expressly
permitted by law, by licence or under terms agreed with the appropriate
reprographics rights organization. Enquiries concerning reproduction outside
the scope of the above should be sent to the ELT Rights Department, Oxford
University Press, at the address above

You must not circulate this work in any other form and you must impose
this same condition on any acquirer

Links to third party websites are provided by Oxford in good faith and for
information only. Oxford disclaims any responsibility for the materials
contained in any third party website referenced in this work

ISBN: 978 0 19 455902 7

Printed in China

This book is printed on paper from certified and well-managed sources

ACKNOWLEDGEMENTS

Illustrations by: Judy Brown pp.7, 12 (Ex 1), 18 (Ex 1), 19 (Ex 4), 21, 25, 27, 32, 35, 39 (Ex 6), 44, 50, 64 (Ex 15), 72 (Ex 1), 84, 88, 92 (Ex 1), 98 (Ex 1), 109, 111, 116 (Ex 2), 117 (Ex 5), 124, 130, 133, 134 (Ex 8), 143, 148 (Ex 1), 151, 153 (Ex 11), 154; Heather Clarke pp.8 (Ex 1), 10 (Ex 5), 14, 16, 18 (Ex 18), 23 (Ex 5), 26, 29 (Ex 3), 56 (Ex 11), 67, 74, 76 (Ex 3), 79 (Ex 1), 80, 85 (Ex 7), 86 (bee etc), 96 (Ex 1), 97, 99, 104, 112, 114 (Ex 6), 123, 126 (Ex 5), 131, 142, 145 (Ex 2), 146, 149 (Ex 3&4), 150 (Ex 2), 155 (Ex 16), 156 (Ex 6); James Hart/Sylvie Poggio Artists Agency pp.10 (Ex 8), 12 (Ex 4), 20, 23 (Ex 6), 34 (Ex 1), 37, 39 (Ex 7), 41, 43, 48, 52, 55, 57, 70, 77, 86 (Ex 3), 93 (Ex 3), 94, 114 (Ex 4), 116 (Ex 3), 126 (Ex 6), 138 (Ex 5), 141 (Ex 9), 149 (Ex 5), 150 (Ex 3), 152 (Ex 7), 153 (Ex 12); Sean Longcroft pp.9, 19 (Ex 6), 22, 38 (Ex 2), 49, 51, 58, 61 (Ex 6), 69, 73, 75, 81 (Ex 6), 82, 83 (Ex 1), 87 (Ex 3), 89, 90, 102, 119, 125, 129, 132 (Ex 1), 136, 138 (Ex 4), 147, 155 (Ex 14), 156 (Ex 14); Andy Peters pp.6, 8 (shelves), 13, 17, 24, 29 (bike), 31, 34 (See, hear, smell), 35, 40, 42, 46, 53, 56 (the phone rang), 59 (Ex 3), 60, 62, 64 (a cold), 66 (fire-eater), 68, 72 (library), 78 (interview), 79 (skateboard), 81 (Can and could), 83 (balloon), 85 (May), 87 (garden), 91, 92 (house), 95 (Ex 4), 98 (picture), 101, 103, 105, 106, 108, 115, 117 (prepositions), 120, 121, 126 (Ex 7), 127, 132 (house), 134 (funny film), 135, 139, 141 (Because and so), 145 (chameleon), 152 (Ex 10); Alexandria Turner/The Bright Agency pp.15, 19 (Ex 7), 24, 36, 38 (Ex 3), 45, 54, 59 (Ex 1), 61 (Ex 4), 66 (Ex 1), 76 (Ex 1 & 2), 78 (Ex 3), 86 (Ex 4), 93 (Ex 4), 95 (Ex 1&3), 96 (Ex 2), 113, 118, 122, 125, 140, 140, 148 (Ex 2), 152 (Ex 8)

Introduction

Oxford Grammar for Schools helps students develop a detailed understanding of grammar form and use in context, and inspires them to have fun with English through songs and games. The grammar is introduced or revised through easy-to-read tables and illustrated presentations with clear examples. The exercises build from simple concept-check activities up to more communicative and productive skills-based activities. In each unit there are several speaking activities where students work with each other to use English with improved accuracy and confidence. The extended writing activities also encourage students to use language in realistic situations.

Each unit begins with a 'Can do' statement, which says what students will be able to achieve on completion of the unit. At the end of each unit is a self-evaluation table. Students should be encouraged to rate their progress in each exercise, which helps them to take responsibility for their own learning and also increases motivation.

At the end of the book there are four pages of extra information for the information gap activities, a word list, and an irregular verb list.

Students can use the *Oxford Grammar for Schools* series in class with their coursebook to support and reinforce their grammar study. The Teacher's Book includes all the answers and audio scripts. There are also tests for every Student's Book unit, and review tests which can be used at the end of a school term.

Student's DVD-ROM

The Student's DVD-ROM includes scored interactive activities as well as all the Student's Book pages in digital form and all the listening exercises and songs. The Student's DVD-ROM enables students to use the Student's Book outside class, and can also be used on an interactive whiteboard in class.

Key to the symbols

▶ 0.0 0.0 (=track number)	Listening activity
(speech bubble)	Speaking activity
GAME	Game
(pencil)	Extended writing activity
(ear)	Pronunciation activity
♪ ♪ ♪	Song
*	Introductory exercise
**	Moderately challenging exercise
***	Most challenging exercise

A difficulty rating is given to each exercise. The scale of difficulty is relative to each unit, so there are exercises with one, two, and three stars in every unit.

Contents

1	Subject and object pronouns	Subject pronouns Object pronouns	6
2	Plurals	Regular plurals; spelling rules and pronunciation Irregular plurals	8
Mini-revision Units 1–2			12
3	Articles and quantifiers	**A**, **an** and **some**; singular and plural countable nouns; uncountable nouns **There is** and **There are** **How much**, **how many**, **some**, **any** and **a lot of**; expressions with containers	13
4	Demonstratives	Demonstrative adjectives **this**, **that**, **these**, **those**; with and without a noun	17
Mini-revision Units 3–4			21
Revision 1 Units 1–4			22
5	**Make**	**Make somebody** or **something** + adjective **Make somebody** or **something** + verb **Be made of** + noun	24
6	Verb patterns: **love**, **like**, **hate** and **want**	Verb + **-ing** form Verb + **to** + base form	29
7	Verbs of sensation	**See**, **hear**, **smell** **Look** + adjective; **look like** + noun	34
Revision 2 Units 5–7			38
8	Present simple and continuous	Uses of the present simple; adverbs of frequency **Have got** Uses of the present continuous; time expressions Present simple and continuous contrast	40
9	Past simple	**Was**, **were**; past time expressions Past simple regular verbs Past simple irregular verbs	46
10	Past continuous	Use of the past continuous to give background information Past continuous and past simple contrast; simultaneous and interrupted past events	53
Mini-revision Units 8–10			59
11	Present perfect	Present perfect for past events, experiences and situations Present perfect and past simple contrast **Since** and **for**	60
12	The future	**Will** and **be going to**	66
13	Imperatives	Warnings, instructions, directions	72
Mini-revision Units 11–13			76
Revision 3 Units 8–13			77
14	**Can** and **could** for ability and permission	**Can** and **could** for ability **Can** and **could** for permission	79
15	**Might** and **may**	**Might** and **may** for possibility **May** for permission	83

4   Contents

Mini-revision	Units 14–15		86
16	**Have to**, **must** and **shall**	**Have to** and **don't have to** **Must** and **mustn't**; obligation, prohibition and necessity **Shall** for offers	87
17	**Should**	**Should** and **shouldn't**; opinions and advice	92
Mini-revision	Units 16–17		95
Revision 4	**Units 16–18**		**96**
18	Adjectives	Adjective agreement; position with verbs and nouns; plurals; articles **Look** and **look like** Adjective order before a noun	98
19	Adverbs	**Already**, **quickly**, **always** Adverbs of manner Adverbs of frequency Adverbs of time: **still**, **yet**, **already**	103
20	Comparative and superlative adjectives	Comparative adjectives Superlative adjectives	108
Revision 5	**Units 18–20**		**113**
21	Prepositions of place	**In**, **on**, and **at** Other prepositions of place	115
22	Prepositions of time	**In**, **on**, and **at** Time expressions	120
Revision 6	**Unit 21–22**		**125**
23	Question words	**Who**, **where**, **what**, **when**, **why**, **how** **Who** as subject; word order Questions with **what** + noun and **how** + adjective/adverb	127
24	Question tags	Question tags in conversation Question tags to check information	132
Revision 7	**Units 23–24**		**137**
27	Conjunctions	**And**, **but**, **or**, **because** and **so**	139
28	Zero conditional	Condition and result clauses	145
Revision 8	**Units 25–26**		**148**
Revision 9	**All units**		**150**

Extra information — **154**

Word list — **158**

Irregular verb list — **160**

1 Subject and object pronouns

I can recognize and use subject and object pronouns.

We use subject and object pronouns like this:

Subject	Verb	Object
The artist	painted	Jack and Heidi.
He	*painted*	**them**.
Jack and Heidi	like	the picture.
They	*like*	**it**.

	Subject pronouns	Object pronouns
Singular	I you he she it	me you him her it
Plural	we you they	us you them

***1 Complete the sentences with subject pronouns.**

▶ Mary has a dog.
   <u>She</u> has a dog.
1 Emily and Paul are here.
   _____ 're here.
2 Andy speaks Russian.
   <u>He</u> speaks Russian.
3 The pens are new.
   _____ 're new.
4 Dave and I like tennis.
   _____ like tennis.
5 The house is very old.
   _____ 's very old.
6 My sister's late.
   _____ 's late.

***2 Complete the sentences with object pronouns.**

▶ I can see Tom and Louise.
   I can see <u>them</u>.
1 I know that man.
   I know <u>him</u>.
2 I work with Anna Jackson.
   I work with <u>her</u>.
3 Suzy loved the flowers.
   Suzy loved <u>it</u>.
4 You can come with George and me.
   You can come with <u>us</u>.
5 This book is for you, Dave, and for you, Vicky.
   This book is for _____.
6 You can open the letter.
   You can open _____.

6 Subject and object pronouns

3 Choose the correct answer.

▶ I've got (them) / they.
1. Can you help us / we?
2. Him / He lives here.
3. They / Them are German.
4. He doesn't know me / I.
5. I can go with she / her.
6. I / Me drink juice in the morning.

4 Write the sentences in the correct order.

▶ her / he / remembers
   He remembers her.
1. them / they / like
   _____
2. teaches / he / us
   _____
3. it / helps / me
   _____
4. they / can hear / him
   _____
5. I / them / want
   _____
6. her / it / confuses
   _____

5 ▶ 1.1 What are they talking about? Listen and number 1–5.

 a
 d
 b
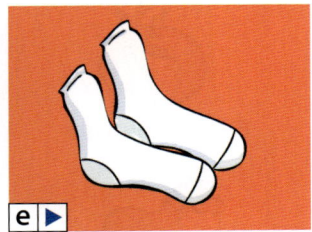 e ▶
 c
 f

6 ▶ 1.2 Complete the sentences with subject and object pronouns. Then listen and check.

▶ You wear *them* on your feet. *They* keep your feet warm.
1. _____'s in the sky. At night, _____'s yellow.
2. _____ live in fields and on farms. People ride _____.
3. _____ rules a country. You see _____ on coins and stamps.
4. _____'s small. _____'s green. _____ will change into a butterfly one day.
5. _____ keeps _____ safe in the car.

7 Look at exercises 5 and 6. Complete the sentences with the words in the box. Use a dictionary if you need to!

| a seatbelt   a queen   the moon |
| ~~a caterpillar~~   socks   horses |

Picture a It's *a caterpillar*.
Picture b They're _____.
Picture c She's _____.
Picture d It's _____.
Picture e They're _____.
Picture f It's _____.

Self-evaluation Rate your progress.

	😊	😊😊	😊😊😊
1			
2			
3			
4			
5			
6			
7			

Unit 1

2 Plurals

I can recognize, form and use regular and irregular plurals.

Regular plurals

I've got four **shelves**, six **books** and ten **trophies**!

We add **-s** to most nouns to form the plural.
tree   ship   flower   cat   shell
tree**s**   ship**s**   flower**s**   cat**s**   shell**s**

Here are some more regular spelling rules.

Add **-es** to nouns ending in **-s, -ss, -sh, -ch, -x,** and **-o.**	
bus	bus**es**
dress	dress**es**
box	box**es**
potato	potato**es**

Change **-y** to **-ies** in nouns ending in consonant + **-y.**	
pony	pon**ies**
family	famil**ies**

Change **-fe** to **-ves.**	
wife	wi**ves**
shelf	shel**ves**

Add just **-s** to nouns ending in vowel + **-y.**	
key	key**s**
toy	toy**s**

*1 ▶ 2.1 Look at the pictures. Write the plurals. Listen and check, then listen and repeat.

▶ one hat   two _hats_

1 one face   two _faces_

2 one knife   two _knive_

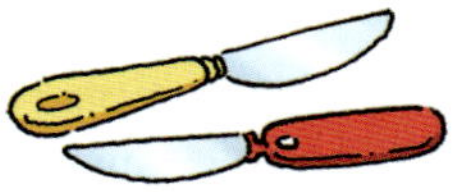

3 one brush   two _brushs_

4 one leaf   two _leafs_

5 one fly   two _flies_

6 one tomato   two _tomatoes_

7 one donkey   two _donkeys_

8 one apple   two _apples_

8   Plurals

*2 2.2 **Listen and repeat.**
/z/: flowers, potatoes, ponies, keys, shelves   /s/: cats, rocks, ships   /ɪz/: buses, dresses, boxes

*3 2.3 **Listen to the final sound in these plurals. What sound do you hear? Draw lines from the words to the sounds.**

flowers noses weeks cars fives places hats lips brushes cups doors horses books pages rooms

Irregular plurals

These nouns have irregular plural forms.

man, woman, child, tooth, foot

men, women, children, teeth, feet

fish, sheep, mouse, goose, person

fish, sheep, mice, geese, people

piano, radio, photo

pianos, radios, photos

*4 2.4 **Change the singular sentences to plural sentences. Listen and check, then listen and repeat.**

▶ I'm a man.
   They're _men_.
1 It's a mouse.
   They're _mice_.
2 It's a photo.
   They're _photos_.
3 She's a child.
   They're _children_.

4 He has one tooth.
   I have thirty _teeth_.
5 He has one fish.
   I have six _fish_.
6 I can see one woman.
   He can see four _women_.
7 You can see one person.
   I can see three _people_.

8 This is a radio.
   These are _radios_.
9 Ow! My foot!
   Ow! My _feet_!
10 One sheep.
   One hundred _sheeps_!

Unit 2   9

5 ▶ 2.5 Listen and tick the correct picture.

6 Write the singular form.

▶ one _foot_, two feet
1. one _____, three geese
2. one _____, four wives
3. one _____, five addresses
4. one _____, six stories
5. one _____, seven scarves
6. one _____, eight pianos
7. one _____, nine mosquitoes
8. one _____, ten children
9. one _____, eleven wolves
10. one _____, twelve strawberries

7 GAME Work in pairs and make true sentences about the numbers below. How many sentences can you make?

7 24 100 365
4 12 31 30
28 160 8 60 26

"There are seven colours in a rainbow."

"There are 12 months in a year."

8 GAME Work in pairs. Find ten more differences between picture 1 and picture 2.

"In picture 1 I can see three chairs but in picture 2 I can see four chairs."

"In picture 2 I can see two windows but in picture 1 I can see one window."

Picture 1

Picture 2

10 Plurals

9 Correct the spelling mistakes.

▶ All classs start at 9 o'clock.
classes

1 Donkies: this way
_____

2 Ponys: this way
_____

3 My photoes
_____

4 Adults £5.00, Childern: Free
_____

5 Danger! Wolfs
_____

6 Cherrys: £4 per kilo
_____

7 Toothbrushs: £1.50
_____

8 Potatos: 70p per kilo
_____

9 Sandwichs: £3.50, Cakes: £4.00
_____

10 Complete the plurals in the questionnaire. Then ask your partner the questions and write their answers.

CLOTHES QUESTIONNAIRE

▶ How many rings__ do you have?   0

1 How many pairs of jean__ do you have?   __

2 How many pairs of sunglass__ do you have?   __

3 How many pairs of sock__ do you have?   __

4 How many necklace__ do you have?   __

5 How many dress__ do you have?   __

6 How many hat__ do you have?   __

7 How many watch__ do you have?   __

8 How many glove__ do you have?   __

Self-evaluation Rate your progress.

	😊	😊😊	😊😊😊
1			
2			
3			
4			
5			
6			
7			
8			
9			
10			

Unit 2   11

Mini-revision Units 1–2

Reading and writing

1 Read the email. Choose the correct words from the box and write them next to 1–5.

> child children ~~family~~ families her
> men man she woman women

I have a big _family_. There are lots of
¹_____ – my mum, my three older sisters, my two aunts and my grandma. There's just one ²_____ – my dad. My oldest sister is married. She's got two girls and two boys. That's four ³_____! My grandma is lovely. ⁴_____ is 79 years old. We call ⁵_____ 'Granny Rose'.

2 Read the letter and write the missing words. Write one word on each line.

> Dear Ben,
>
> Thank you for your letter. _It_ arrived yesterday. The photos are great! I look at ¹_____ every day. How is your brother? Is ²_____ still in hospital? Please say 'hello' to ³_____ from me. Write to ⁴_____ again soon. Or maybe we can speak on the phone some time?
> I can call ⁵_____.
>
> From
> Andy

Listening

3 ▶ R1.1 Listen and write.

▶ How does Harry travel to school?
   by bus

1 What does Harry see?
   _____

2 Who is on the bus in the morning?
   _____

3 Who does Harry talk to?
   _____

4 Who does Harry travel home with?
   _____

5 Who does Harry meet at the bus stop?
   _____

Speaking

4 Work in pairs. Look at the pictures. Can you find 10 differences?

Picture 1

Picture 2

> In Picture 1 the bird is brown but in Picture 2 it's white.

12 Units 1–2

3 Articles and quantifiers

I can identify and use countable and uncountable nouns; I can use **some**, **any** and **a lot of** with countable and uncountable nouns.

A, an and some

How much fruit is there in the fridge?

There's a melon, there are two apples and there are about 10 oranges.

Most nouns have singular and plural forms. These are countable nouns.

cup → cups   table → tables   child → children

We can use **a**, **some** or a number before countable nouns.

Singular	Plural
a bottle	some bottles
one bottle	six bottles

Some nouns only have one form. These are uncountable nouns.
milk, homework, juice, butter

We can't count uncountable nouns, so we can't use numbers with them. We use **some** or nothing before them.
*I always do **some** homework after school.*
*Do you want **mayonnaise** on your sandwich?*

In positive sentences, we use **there is** and **there are** like this:

There is … +	There are … +
singular countable nouns	plural countable nouns

There's an apple.   *There are bananas.*
There's a bus.   *There are cars.*

There is … +
uncountable nouns

There's fruit.
There's traffic.

✱1 Write C (countable) or U (uncountable).

▶ hospital C
1 toothpaste ___
2 pencil ___
3 spoon ___
4 jam ___
5 necklace ___
6 plan ___
7 salt ___
8 time ___
9 money ___
10 petrol ___
11 cup ___
12 friend ___
13 rain ___
14 sugar ___
15 bread ___
16 star ___
17 lesson ___
18 coffee ___
19 river ___
20 clock ___
21 jewellery ___
22 traffic ___
23 piece ___
24 juice ___
25 furniture ___
26 tea ___
27 box ___

✱✱2 ▶ 3.1 Circle the correct answer. Listen and check, then listen and repeat.

▶ There's **a** / **some** bread in the bag.
1 I can see some **bird** / **birds**.
2 There's **a snow** / **snow** on those mountains.
3 There **'s** / **are** two men on the boat.
4 Would you like **some** / **an** ice in your drink?
5 I want **some** / **two** free time.
6 You've got **a tomato sauce** / **tomato sauce** on your face!
7 I love **rain** / **a rain**!
8 This furniture **is** / **are** very nice.

Unit 3   13

Quantifiers: how much, how many, some, any and a lot of

We use quantifiers to talk about the quantity of countable and uncountable nouns.

Quantifiers	
Countable	Uncountable
How **many**…? some (not) any a lot of 1, 2, 3…	How **much**…? some (not) any a lot of

We usually use **some** in positive sentences and **any** in questions and negatives.

I've got **some** paper and pens.
Have you got **any** money with you?
There isn't **any** butter.

We use **a lot of** with countable and uncountable nouns to talk about a large quantity. We can use it in affirmative and negative sentences and also in questions.

He's got **a lot of** friends.
We haven't got **a lot of** time.
Is there **a lot of** paper in that box?

With uncountable nouns we often use expressions with bottles and containers, like **a bottle of** and **a kilo of**.

He has **a spoonful of** sugar in his coffee.
There are **two bottles of** milk in the fridge.

	a *some* *1, 2, 3*	Countable noun (measurement or container)	*of*	Uncountable noun
I have	two	bags	of	sugar.
I'd like	a	spoonful	of	honey.
There are	100	kilos	of	rice.
There's	a	loaf	of	bread.
I've got	two	litres	of	milk.

Here are some common examples.

a litre of water/petrol/apple juice

a kilo of cheese/beef/potatoes

a bottle of water/lemonade

a tin of beans/fruit/soup/paint

a spoonful of sugar/salt/spice

a tube of toothpaste/glue

a cup of coffee/tea/milk

a jar of jam/honey

a slice of bread/cheese/cake

a bag of biscuits/crisps/flour/rice

*3 Circle the correct answer.

▶ I've got **some** / **any** biscuits.
1 I can see **some** / **any** stars.
2 Why aren't there **some** / **any** chairs in here?
3 I'd like **some** / **any** coffee, please.
4 I need **some** / **any** money.
5 Are there **some** / **any** pictures in that book?
6 I can't hear **some** / **any** birds.
7 We never get **some** / **any** snow in this country.
8 I need **some** / **any** help!
8 There aren't **some** / **any** biscuits left.

14 Articles and quantifiers

4 ▶ 3.2 Listen and tick ✓ the correct picture of Millville.

5 ▶ 3.3 Listen again and tick ✓ the box.

▶ There ___ good shops.
- a aren't any
- ✓ b are a lot of
- c are some

1 You ___ mountains.
- a can see a lot of
- b can't see any
- c can see some

2 There ___ big parks.
- a are a lot of
- b are some
- c aren't any

3 There ___ traffic.
- a 's some
- b isn't any
- c 's a lot of

4 There ___ pollution.
- a isn't any
- b 's some
- c 's a lot of

6 Match the quantities and the nouns.

bottle ~~cup~~ jar litre bag spoonful slice tin tube

▶ a _cup_ of tea
1 a _____ of toothpaste
2 a _____ of flour
3 a _____ of honey
4 a _____ of sugar
5 a _____ of bread
6 a _____ of water
7 a _____ of juice
8 a _____ of beans

7 Work in pairs. Cover your answers in exercise 6. How many phrases can you remember?

(a cup of tea)   (a tube of …)

8 Complete the second sentence so that it means the same as the first.

▶ How many tins of soup are there?
  How _much soup is_ there?

1 How many litres of juice are there?
  How _____ there?

2 How many slices of cake are there?
  How _____ there?

3 How many bags of rice are there?
  How _____ there?

4 How many bottles of water are there?
  How _____ there?

5 How many tins of paint are there?
  How _____ there?

6 How many pieces of fruit are there?
  How _____ there?

7 How many jars of jam are there?
  How _____ there?

8 How many loaves of bread are there?
  How _____ there?

9 How many kilos of flour are there?
  How _____ there?

Unit 3 15

9 GAME Memory game. Look at the picture for one minute, then turn to page 154 and answer the questions.

10 ▶ 3.4 Complete the conversations with *some* or *any*, then listen and check. Act out the conversations with a partner.

▶ 💬 Have you got _any_ family in other countries?
💬 No, but I've got _some_ friends in Italy.

1 💬 I need _____ old family photos for a school project.
💬 There are _____ old photos in that box.

2 💬 Have you got _____ gold jewellery?
💬 No. I've got _____ silver rings but I haven't got _____ gold jewellery.

3 💬 I need _____ shampoo. Can I use _____ of yours?
💬 I haven't got _____, but you can have _____ of my soap.

11 Work in groups. What have you got? Make sentences with quantifiers.

comics magazines free time
pop music classical music
friends in other countries
glitter clay ink charcoal

💬 I've got some comics.

💬 I haven't got any comics but I've got a lot of magazines.

12 Write about two of the things and places below. Include information about the nouns.

My bedroom
bed wardrobe other furniture books DVDs
pictures on the walls

My bag
books tissues pens rubbish bottle of water
food

My town
traffic green spaces cafés shops pollution

My life
friends plans for the future free time

MY BEDROOM
My bedroom is quite small. There's a bed and a wardrobe but there isn't any other furniture. There are some ...

Self-evaluation Rate your progress.

	😊	😊😊	😊😊😊
1			
2			
3			
4			
5			
6			
7			
8			
9			
10			
11			
12			

 Articles and quantifiers

4 Demonstratives

I can recognize and use demonstrative adjectives and pronouns.

This and **these** indicate nouns that are near us.

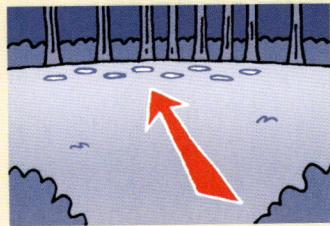

Look at **this**!    What are **these** mushrooms?

That and **those** indicate nouns that are far from us.

Look at **those** footprints!    Can you hear **that** noise?

Demonstrative adjective + noun

We can use **this**, **that**, **these** and **those** with a noun.

This song is really good.
Who's **that** girl?
I want **these** pens.
Those bags are nice.

Demonstrative pronoun + no noun

We can use **this**, **that**, **these** and **those** without a noun when the idea of the noun is clear to the listener or reader.

That's my sister.
What does **this** mean?
Can you post **those** for me?
These are my new glasses.

Unit 4   17

* **1** ▶ 4.1 Listen and number the conversations 1–6.

a ☐

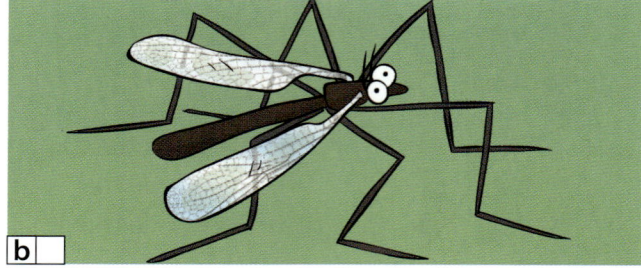
b ☐

c ☐

d ☐

e 1

f ☐

* **2** Complete the sentences with *is* or *are*.

▶ What *is* this?
1 These chocolates _____ nice.
2 Those men _____ tall.
3 What _____ those?
4 This exercise _____ difficult.
5 These mice _____ small.
6 This _____ interesting.
7 That _____ my teacher.
8 Who _____ that?

** **3** ▶ 4.2 Listen. Are the underlined sounds the same or different? Write *S* or *D*. Then listen and repeat.

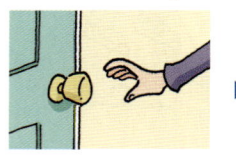
▶ this is the door   S

▶ those ducks   D

1 these things   ___

2 that zebra   ___

3 This is the key.   ___

4 Those are their dogs.   ___

5 Are these vases?   ___

6 That's the bathroom.   ___

18   Demonstrative pronouns

4 ▶ 4.3 Complete the conversations with *this*, *that*, *these* or *those*. Then listen and check.

▶ How much is <u>this</u> hat?
1 _____ fish are beautiful!
2 What are _____ red flowers?
3 Mmm! _____ are delicious!
4 What does _____ sign say?
5 Could you help me with _____ boxes?

5 **GAME** Cover the sentences in exercise 5. Look at the pictures. Can you remember all the sentences with *this*, *that*, *these* and *those*?

How much is that hat?   It's £7.

6 Change these pictures into pictures of your friends and family. Then use *this* and *that* to tell a partner about the people in the pictures.

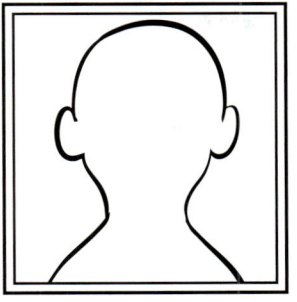
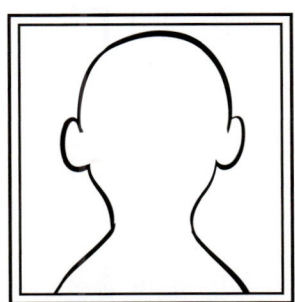
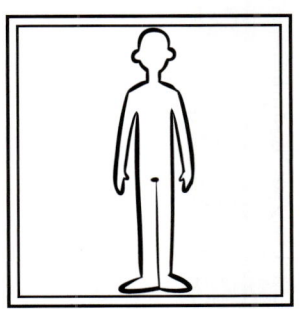

This is my mum and this is my grandpa. He's my mum's dad.

That's my brother, William. He wears glasses.   Who's that?

7 **GAME** Work in pairs. How many parts of the body can you name? Ask and answer with *this*, *that*, *these* and *those*.

What's this?   It's your nose.

What are those?   They're my feet.

Unit 4   19

8 Work in pairs. Act out a conversation between a buyer and a seller at a charity sale. Look at the information below.

HELP OUR SCHOOL!!

Student A, seller
Look at the things on the table. What are they? Decide on prices.
Think carefully! You want to sell lots of things and you want to make lots of money.

These are only £2!   *That CD is really good.*

Student B, buyer
Look at the things on the table. What do you want to buy? What do you want to ask about?
Think carefully! You want to buy the things but you don't want to pay high prices!

What are those books?

This one is 'Birds' and this one is 'Visit China'.

How much is this?   *It's only £1.*

Self-evaluation Rate your progress.

	😊	😊😊	😊😊😊
1			
2			
3			
4			
5			
6			
7			
8			

20 Demonstrative pronouns

Mini-revision Units 3–4

Reading and writing

1 Look and read. Choose the correct words and write them on the lines.

Australia chairs ~~drinks~~ furniture
leaves milk pages Switzerland

▶ These are often made with water. They're hot or cold. drinks

1 You find these in a book. They're white and they have lots of words on them. ____________

2 This is a drink. It's white. ____________

3 This is a country. It's got a lot of mountains. It hasn't got any sea. ____________

4 You find these on trees and other plants. They're green. ____________

5 People have this in their homes. It's often big and heavy. ____________

2 Read the notice. Choose the right words and write them on the lines.

Attention: all artists!

We need some volunteers to help paint a large picture on [1]______ school wall on Saturday morning.

Are you interested? Please read [2]______ notes:

- Wear [3]______ clothes. This is important! There will be [4]______ wet paint and we don't want [5]______ accidents.
- Bring [6]___ food for lunch and [7]______ bottle of water.
- And finally, please tell your friends! We need [8]______ help!

▶	any	a	(some)
1	the	some	any
2	those	this	these
3	a	old	that
4	a lot of	much	many
5	some	any	much
6	some	a	any
7	some	a	any
8	much	many	a lot of

Listening

3 R2.1 What do Julia and her family have for breakfast? Listen and write a letter in each box.

▶ Julia	e	3 Mum	☐	6 Seth	☐
1 Grandpa	☐	4 Dad	☐	7 James	☐
2 Grandma	☐	5 Beth	☐		

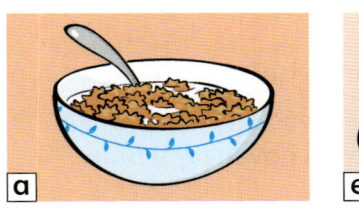

a

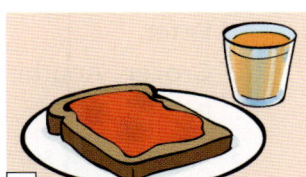

e

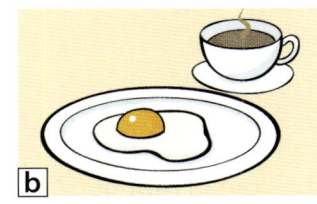

b

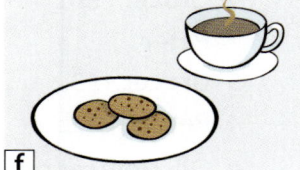

f

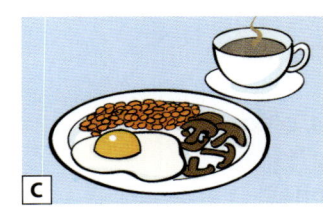

c

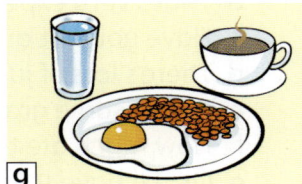

g

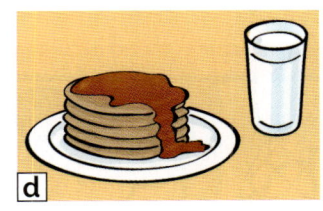

d

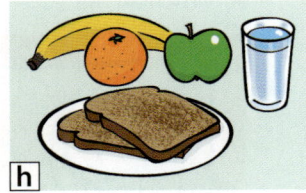

h

Speaking

4 Work in pairs. Ask and answer questions about things in the classroom. Use the questions below.

What's this? What are these?
What's that? What are those?

What are these?
They're pens.
What's that?
It's glue.

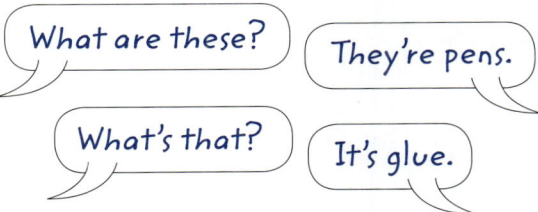

Revision 1 — Units 1–4

Reading and writing

1 What does Peter say to the grocer? Match 1–5 with a letter (a–h). You don't need to use all the letters.

▶ Grocer Can I help you?
  Peter   _e_
1 Grocer These are very sweet.
  Peter   ___
2 Grocer Anything else?
  Peter   ___
3 Grocer No, sorry, I haven't got any.
  Peter   ___
4 Grocer Six.
  Peter   ___
5 Grocer £3.
  Peter   ___

a Oh. How many lemons are in that bag?
b That's very expensive!
c Have you got any apples?
d There's lots of juice.
e I'd like some grapes, please.
f How much are they?
g OK, I'll have those ones.
h What's this?

2 Look and read. Choose the correct words and write them on the lines.

> stories litter wives knives
> mice ~~children~~ jewellery letters

▶ They are very young people. _children_
1 Some people drop this in the street. It's dirty. _____
2 A postman delivers these. _____
3 These small animals eat cheese and other pieces of food. Cats catch them. _____
4 A lot of women wear this. It is often very expensive. _____
5 They're women. Husbands have them! _____
6 People write them and tell them. You can read them in books and magazines. _____
7 They're sharp. You cut fruit, bread, meat and vegetables with them. _____

3 Read the email and write the missing words. Write one word on each line.

Dear Toby

I live with my parents, my brother and my two sisters. _We_ live in a small village called Hanbridge. Hanbridge has got three sheep farms – you can see a ¹_____ of sheep in the fields around here! The village has got a supermarket and a café but ²_____ hasn't got a cinema. And there aren't ³_____ bookshops or music shops, unfortunately.

Write and tell ⁴_____ about your hometown.

Iris

P.S. I'm writing ⁵_____ email on my new computer!

22 Units 1–4

Listening

4 ▶ R3.1 Listen and write.

Mixed Fruit Smoothie

What is it? a delicious <u>snack</u>

Good points healthy and doesn't take much [1]_____

Ingredient 1 a handful of [2]_____

Ingredient 2 some other [3]_____ of fruit – e.g. banana or peach

Ingredient 3 a small pot of [4]_____

Ingredient 4 a [5]_____ of honey

How do you make it? Blend all the ingredients in a food processor for 30 seconds – then enjoy!

5 ▶ R3.2 Listen and tick ✓ the correct picture.

▶ What has Bev got?

a ☐   b ✓   c ☐

1 What weather do they usually have on the island?

a ☐   b ☐   c ☐

2 Which is Bev's grandma?

a ☐   b ☐   c ☐

3 Which is the Island Hotel?

a ☐   b ☐   c ☐

Speaking

6 Look at the pictures and tell the story.

1   4

2   5

3

The two men are hungry. They look in the fridge …

7 Talk with a partner. Which of these do you have in your town or city?

a university   an airport   crime
a bookshop   good clothes shops
young people   traffic   litter   pollution
fresh air   a cinema   a hospital   a river

There isn't a river in this town.

This town has got some good clothes shops.

It's got a university.

There isn't much crime.

Revision 1   23

5 Make

I can recognize and use **make** to mean different things in different verb patterns.

Make somebody or something + adjective

We use **make somebody** or **something** + adjective to describe how an event, action, person or object changes another person or object.
This music's **making me happy**.   Salty food **makes people thirsty**.

*1 ▶ **5.1 Complete the sentences. Use** *make* **or** *makes* **and the adjectives in the box. Then listen and check.**

> angry   calm and relaxed   happy   tired   wet   ~~yellow~~

▶ They _make_ everything _yellow_ .

1 Water _____ things _____ .

2 Exercise _____ me _____ .

3 Yoga _____ people _____ .

4 Bad drivers _____ him _____ .

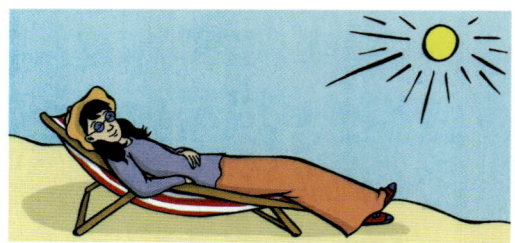

5 The sun _____ her _____ .

24   Make

2 ▶ 5.2 Listen and number the pictures 1–5.

 a ▶
 c
 e
 b
 d
 f

3 ▶ 5.3 Listen again and circle the correct object.

▶ Those will make **me** / **you** ill.
1 It makes **food** / **people** sweet.
2 They make **her** / **me** angry.
3 It makes **us** / **you** thirsty.
4 These make **us** / **you** strong.
5 These things make **everyone** / **people** fat.

4 Write the words in the correct order.

▶ hungry / makes / swimming / me
  Swimming makes me hungry.

1 makes / chocolate / ill / me

2 angry / makes / pollution / me

3 sad / classical music / me / makes

4 happy / football / me / makes

5 me / hot weather / makes / tired

6 me / make / calm and relaxed / yoga

5 Are the sentences in exercise 4 true for you? Talk about your answers with a partner.

Swimming makes me hungry. That's true for me.

It isn't true for me.

6 Match 1–5 with a–f.

▶ I don't read those books at night. _b_
1 Take this medicine three times a day. ___
2 My brothers love snow. ___
3 I put red chilli pepper in all my food. ___
4 My sister doesn't like hospitals. ___
5 I don't like that girl. ___

a It will make you better.
b They make me scared.
c It makes them very happy.
d She makes me really angry.
e They make her sad.
f It makes it hot and spicy.

7  Work in pairs. Cover 1–5 in exercise 6. Read sentences a–f. Can you remember sentences 1–5?

Unit 5   25

Make somebody or something + verb

> We use **make somebody** or **something** + verb to describe how an event or action creates a second event or action.
> That **made me jump**.

8 ▶ **5.4 Listen and tick ✓ the sentence that is true.**

- ▶ ☐ He made her shout.
  ✓ He made her jump.
- 1 ☐ She made him stop.
  ☐ She made him go.
- 2 ☐ He made the bird fly away.
  ☐ He made the woman go away.
- 3 ☐ The book made her cry.
  ☐ The book made her laugh.
- 4 ☐ She made him fall off his bike.
  ☐ She didn't make him fall off his bike.
- 5 ☐ The pepper made the woman sneeze.
  ☐ The pepper made everyone sneeze.
- 6 ☐ The dogs are making them smile.
  ☐ They are making the dogs dance.

9 ▶ **5.5 Answer these two questions about pronunciation. Then listen and repeat the sentence.**

1 Which word in the coloured sentence has the main stress? <u>Underline</u> it.

   He made her jump.

2 What kind of word is the underlined word?
   - ☐ the subject
   - ☐ make
   - ☐ the object
   - ☐ the verb

10 Look at the pictures and complete the sentences. Use *'s making*, *are making*, an object and a verb.

Objects
~~her~~   her   him   them   the puppet   the wheel

Verbs
cry   dance   laugh   ~~smile~~   sneeze   spin

- ▶ The book's *making her smile*.
- 1 The onions _____.
- 2 The clowns _____.
- 3 The boy _____.
- 4 The flowers _____.
- 5 The man _____.

11 GAME Work in pairs. Cover the sentences in exercise 10 and look at the pictures. How many sentences can you remember?

26   Make

Be made of + noun

We use **be made of** + noun to describe objects and their material.
It's made of plastic.

✷12 ▶ 5.6 Look at the pictures and complete the sentences. Use *'s made of* or *'re made of* + a noun from the box. Then listen and check.

Nouns
leather metal glass paper rubber snow ~~wood~~ wool

▶ It*'s made of wood*.
1 They_____.
2 It_____.
3 It_____.
4 They_____.
5 It_____.
6 They_____.
7 It_____.

✷✷✷13  Work in pairs. Cover the sentences in exercise 12 and look at the pictures. How many sentences can you remember?

✷14 ▶ 5.7 Answer these two questions about pronunciation. Then listen again and repeat all the sentences.
1 Which word in the coloured sentence has the main stress? <u>Underline</u> it.
   It's made of wood.
2 What kind of word is the underlined word?
   ☐ the subject   ☐ made   ☐ the noun

✷15 Tick ✓ the sentences that are correct. Correct the sentences that are wrong.
▶ Is he making the children (crying)?
   Is he making the children cry?
1 Will it make you ill?
   _____
2 Is it made in glass?
   _____
3 Did I make you to jump?
   _____
4 Is it make people laugh?
   _____
5 Does it make food hot?
   _____

✷16 **GAME** Work in pairs or groups. Choose an object below. Ask and answer *yes/no* questions to guess each other's objects.

Is it made of metal?   *Yes, it is.*

Unit 5 27

17 GAME Work in teams. Answer as many questions as possible.

Think of three things that …

… are made of wood
pencils tables doors

… are made of metal

… are made of plastic

… are made of leather

… are made of cotton

… make people cry

… make people laugh

… make people sneeze

… make people scream

… make people jump

… make people happy

… make people sad

… make people angry

… make people scared

… make food sweet

… make food spicy

… make dogs happy

… make cats happy

18 Write the words in the correct order to make questions. Then interview a partner.

▶ happy / makes / what / you
  What makes you happy?

1 scared / makes / what / you

2 what / laugh / you / makes

3 makes / angry / what / you

4 made of / shoes / what / your / are

5 made of / what's / your / bag

6 what / sing / you / makes

7 grow / what / makes / you

8 hungry / you / what / makes

Self-evaluation Rate your progress.

	🙂	🙂🙂	🙂🙂🙂
1			
2			
3			
4			
5			
6			
7			
8			
9			
10			
11			
12			
13			
14			
15			
16			
17			
18			

Make

6 Verb patterns: love, like, hate and want

I can use the correct verb forms after **love**, **like**, **hate**, and **want** or **would like** to talk about preferences and desires.

Verb + -ing form

When we use two verbs together, the second verb is sometimes in the **-ing** form and sometimes in the **to** + base form.

Verb 1	Verb 2
He likes	**riding** his bike.
He wants	**to ride** his bike.

I like riding my bike.

I want to ride my bike now!

We make the **-ing** form like this:

Most verbs	Verbs ending in -e (ride, dance)	Verbs ending vowel + consonant (get, swim)
+ **-ing**	remove **-e**, + **-ing**	double the final consonant, + **-ing**
read → reading wait → waiting	ride → riding lose → losing	get → getting swim → swimming

We often use the **-ing** form after the verbs **love**, **like** and **hate**.
Love, like, don't like and **hate** express our general preferences.
We often use **love, like, don't like** and **hate** + **-ing** to talk about our feelings for hobbies and everyday activities.

♥ I **love** play**ing** computer games.
✓ I **like** read**ing** in bed.
✗ I **don't like** be**ing** late for things.
✗✗ I **hate** tidy**ing** my bedroom.

*1 Write the -ing forms.

▶ drink <u>drinking</u>
1 play _____
2 sit _____
3 have _____
4 chat _____
5 go _____
6 do _____
7 win _____
8 run _____
9 get _____
10 tidy _____
11 find _____
12 lose _____
13 clean _____

*2 Complete the text with the -ing form of the verb in brackets.

My sister Daisy and I are very different! She likes <u>doing</u> (do) sports, but I like ¹_____ (make) things. I like ²_____ (draw), ³_____ (paint) and ⁴_____ (cook). I like ⁵_____ (write) stories too. Daisy hates ⁶_____ (be) inside the house. She loves ⁷_____ (swim) in summer and ⁸_____ (ski) in winter.

**3 ⏵ 6.1 Complete the 'You' column with ♥, ✓, ✗ and ✗✗. Then listen to Amy and Fred, and complete the table.

♥ = love ✗ = don't like
✓ = like ✗✗ = hate

	You	Amy	Fred
paint		✓	✗✗
computer games			
basketball			
ball games			

Unit 6 29

4  Write the correct verb in the -ing form next to each noun. Work in pairs. Tell your partner what you like and don't like doing.

| do do go draw get up ~~listen to~~ swim |
| play play read swim take watch |

▶ _listening to_ music
1 _____ in the sea
2 _____ early
3 _____ jigsaw puzzles
4 _____ crossword puzzles
5 _____ pictures
6 _____ magazines
7 _____ films
8 _____ to the supermarket
9 _____ photos
10 _____ board games
11 _____ football

(I like watching films.)

(I don't like doing crossword puzzles.)

5 Write the sentences.

▶ They / love / take / photos
They love taking photos.

1 I / like / chat / online
_____

2 She / like / run
_____

3 I / not like / be / late / for school
_____

4 Tom / love / write / stories
_____

5 I / hate / dance
_____

6 He / not like / go / to the dentist
_____

7 Sally and I / love / act
_____

8 They / not like / sing
_____

9 I / like / be / outdoors
_____

10 She / hate / do / sport
_____

6 How do you, your family and friends feel about the activities below? Write sentences.

Communication
read speak chat online listen
write letters/emails/text messages

Sport
run jump swim ski play golf

Housework
cook clean tidy shop for food

Hobbies
paint draw sing act play watch

COMMUNICATION
I like chatting on the phone. My mum likes writing letters. I don't like writing letters. I like writing emails. I hate ...

7 **GAME** Work in pairs. Take turns to make sentences about the people. The name and a word in the activity start with the same letter. How many lines of three can you get?

(Carla hates making cakes.)

(George doesn't like going shopping.)

(Leo loves listening to music.)

(We've got a line of three!)

Alison ✓	Betty ✓	Carla ✗✗	Dave ♥	Edward ♥
Emma ✓	Frank ♥	George ✗	Jill ✗	Jenny ✗✗
Isabella ✓	Katy ♥	Leo ♥	Libby ✗✗	Molly ✓
Mike ✗	Oscar ✓	Polly ✗	Pat ♥	Robert ✗✗
Sally ♥	Tanya ♥	William ✗	Tony ♥	Yasmin ✗✗

30 Verb patterns: **love, like, hate** and **want**

Verb + to + base form

We use **want** + **to** + base form to talk about a specific wish, desire, goal or ambition for the future. We don't use it to talk about our general preferences and feelings.
*He **wants to be** a doctor.*
*I **don't want to go** home.*

We can also use **would like** + **to** + base form to talk about our hopes and desires. We often use it when we think about the future.
*I'd **like to live** in the mountains.*
*Where **would** you **like to go**?*

*8 ▶ 6.2 Listen and tick ✓ the correct answer.

▶ Sam _____ to go to the supermarket.
  a ✓ doesn't want   b ☐ wants

1 Jenny wants _____ this evening.
  a ☐ to go out   b ☐ to stay at home

2 The woman _____ to sit down.
  a ☐ doesn't want   b ☐ wants

3 Charlie would like to be _____.
  a ☐ a teacher   b ☐ an astronaut

4 Ben _____ like to work in a hospital.
  a ☐ would   b ☐ wouldn't

5 Alex doesn't want _____.
  a ☐ to be rich   b ☐ to be famous

6 Sue _____ speak to the teacher.
  a ☐ wants to   b ☐ doesn't want to

*9 ▶ 6.3 Listen to these sentences. Answer the question about pronunciation. Listen again and repeat the sentences.

I don't want to go to bed.
I want to watch a film.
I don't want to sit down.
Do you want to go out?
I wouldn't like to live here.
Would you like to be a doctor?

How do we pronounce **to** in the sentences above?
a /tuː/
b /tə/

*10 ▶ 6.4 Complete the conversations with the correct form of the verbs in brackets. Then listen and check. Act the conversations with a partner.

▶ 💬 I'd like <u>to go</u> (go) to the beach.
  💬 Me too but I don't want <u>to go</u> (go) in the sea.

1 💬 Do you want _____ (stop) for lunch?
  💬 No, I'm OK, thanks. But I'd like _____ (have) a cold drink.

2 💬 I don't want _____ (go) to school tomorrow.
  💬 Nor me. I don't want _____ (do) that exam.

3 💬 I'd like _____ (have) lots of money!
  💬 Me too! I'd like _____ (be) rich and famous.

*11 What do you want to do? Write sentences with *(don't) want* and *would(n't) like*. Then talk about your sentences in small groups.

invent something   travel around the world
be famous   go to university   go to the moon
live in another country

I want to go to university.

I wouldn't like to go to the moon.

Unit 6   31

12 ▶ 6.5 Read and listen. Match the pictures to words in the song. Listen again and repeat.

1
He loves jumping.
He loves climbing.
He doesn't like lying around.
He'd like to be a pilot
or a high skydiver.
He doesn't want to stay on the ground.

2
She likes thinking.
She likes doing puzzles.
She doesn't like running about.
She'd like to be a scientist or maybe a spy.
She wants to help and sort things out.

3
They both love winning.
They both hate losing.
They don't like getting things wrong.
They want to win a trophy,
a gold medal or a cup.
And they don't want to wait
very long!

13 Work in pairs. Underline all the activities and situations in the song. Circle all the jobs and ambitions. Talk with a partner. Do you feel the same or different to the people in the song?

He doesn't like lying around but I like lying around!

Me too. Would you like to be a pilot?

No. And I wouldn't like to be a skydiver.

14 Read the notice. Write a text for the competition.

Competition: 'My goals in life'

What are your goals?
What would you like to do? Why?

Write and tell us about:
- Your study goals
- Your job goals
- Other goals
- Big prizes for the winners!

*My goals
I'd love to be a vet. I like animals and I love helping people. I want to …*

Verb patterns: **love**, **like**, **hate** and **want**

15 Complete the emails with the *-ing* or *to* + base form of the verb in brackets.

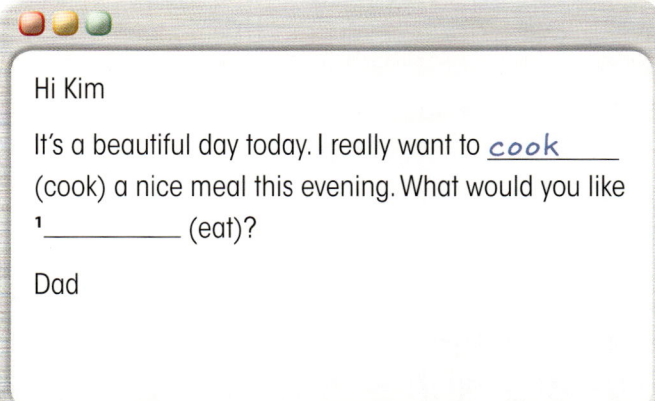

Hi Kim

It's a beautiful day today. I really want to *cook* (cook) a nice meal this evening. What would you like ¹_____ (eat)?

Dad

Dear Kim

Would you like ⁶_____ (go) on holiday with me this year? I like ⁷_____ (travel) to different cities and I love ⁸_____ (visit) museums. How about you? What do you like ⁹_____ (do) on holiday? And where would you like ¹⁰_____ (go)?

Beth

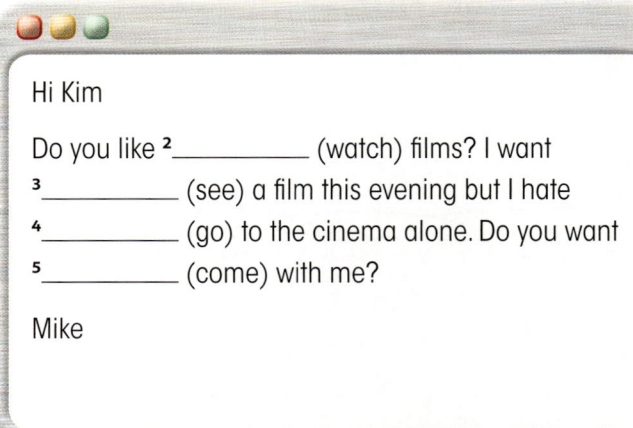

Hi Kim

Do you like ²_____ (watch) films? I want ³_____ (see) a film this evening but I hate ⁴_____ (go) to the cinema alone. Do you want ⁵_____ (come) with me?

Mike

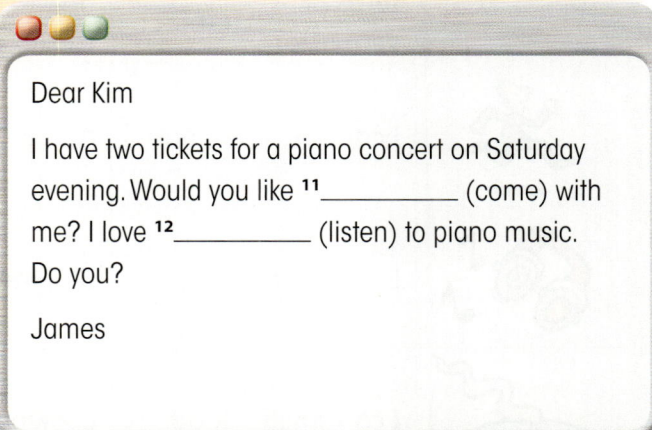

Dear Kim

I have two tickets for a piano concert on Saturday evening. Would you like ¹¹_____ (come) with me? I love ¹²_____ (listen) to piano music. Do you?

James

16 You are Kim. Reply to the emails in exercise 15.

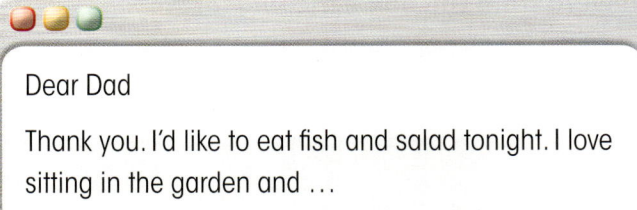

Dear Dad

Thank you. I'd like to eat fish and salad tonight. I love sitting in the garden and …

17 Work in pairs. What do you like doing? What do you want or what would you like to do now?

sleep   play football   eat pizza   be outside
talk to my brother   be at home

I like eating pizza but I don't want to eat pizza now!

I'd like to be outside now.

Self-evaluation Rate your progress.

Unit 6   33

7 Verbs of sensation

I can recognize and use **see**, **hear**, **look**, **sound**, **feel**, **taste** and **smell**.

See, hear, smell

We use **see**, **smell** and **hear** to talk about the sights, smells and sounds that we notice. We usually use **can** with these verbs of sensation. Look at these verb patterns.

	Verb of sensation	Object	-ing form
	I can see	a man	running.
	I can hear	music	playing.
	I can smell	food	cooking.

That man **looks** angry!

Yes, I **can hear** him shouting.

Oh, no… he doesn't **look** angry — he **looks** scared. I **can see** a big animal.

It **looks** like a cow.

No, it's a bull! Run!

*1 Look at the picture. Complete the sentences with a word from the box + the *-ing* form of the verb in brackets.

a dog   a cat   ~~a man~~   a woman   a boy   a policeman   two women

▶ I can see _a man talking_ (talk) on the phone.
1 I can see _____ (sleep) under a tree.
2 I can see _____ (ride) a bike.
3 I can see _____ (paint) a wall.
4 I can see _____ (play) with a toy mouse.
5 I can see _____ (climb) a tree.
6 I can see _____ (eat) a sandwich.

2 🔊 **7.1** What can you hear? Listen and circle the correct answer.

▶ I can hear (a person walking) / a horse running.
1. I can hear someone **singing** / **whistling**.
2. I can hear **a dog barking** / **a bird singing**.
3. I can hear **a clock ticking** / **an alarm ringing**.
4. I can hear **a phone** / **phones** ringing.
5. I can hear **a man** / **a woman** singing.
6. I can hear someone **coughing** / **sneezing**.
7. I can hear people **shouting** / **laughing**.
8. I can hear **a person** / **people** clapping.

3  Talk in small groups. What can you hear? What can you see? What can you smell? Use the nouns and verbs below.

Nouns a dog a clock a plane a bird a person the teacher my friends clouds people food pupils

Verbs bark cook cough laugh move shout sing ring talk tick whistle write

I can hear people talking.

I can see clouds moving.

Look + adjective; look like + noun

We use **look**, **taste**, **smell**, **feel**, **sound** and **seem** to give an opinion about an object, activity or person.
We can use an adjective or **like** + noun with these verbs of sensation. To give an opinion about a feeling, we use a verb of sensation + an adjective.

Subject	Verb of sensation	Adjective
She	sounds	happy.
She	seems	tired.
That	looks	interesting.

To say that a thing or person is similar to another thing or a person, we use a verb of sensation + noun.

Subject	Verb of sensation	Like	Noun
He	looks	like	my brother.
This	tastes	like	honey.
It	feels	like	plastic.

You look like a snowman!

I know. But I feel really warm!

4 Look at the pictures and complete the sentences with *look* or *looks* and an adjective from the box.

hot cold sad ~~good~~ funny angry difficult happy

▶ That <u>looks good</u>!
1. He _____.
2. They _____.
3. That _____.
4. She _____.
5. They _____.
6. They _____.
7. He _____.

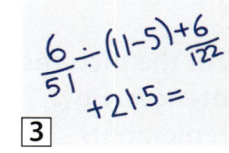

5 Look at the pictures and complete the sentences with *look* or *looks like* and a noun from the box.

a boat   a banana   a bowl of fruit   ~~a car~~
flowers   a frog   stars   an umbrella

▶ It _looks like a car_.
1 It _____.
2 They _____.
3 It _____.
4 They _____.
5 It _____.
6 It _____.
7 It _____.

6 Work with a partner. Look at the pictures in exercise 5. Cover the sentences. How many sentences can you remember?

7 Complete the second sentence so it means the same as the first. Use the adjectives in the box.

bad   calm   ~~good~~   happy
interested   right   sweet

▶ That sounds terrible.
   It doesn't sound _good_.
1 This doesn't smell nice.
   This smells _____.
2 That looks wrong.
   It doesn't look _____.
3 You look sad.
   You don't look very _____.
4 I feel nervous.
   I don't feel _____.
5 This orange tastes bitter.
   It doesn't taste _____.
6 He sounds bored.
   He doesn't sound very _____.

8 Circle the correct answer.
▶ They **look** / **(look like)** football players.
1 I don't **feel** / **feel like** tired. Do you?
2 Excuse me. That **sounds** / **sounds like** my phone.
3 Does that **feel** / **feel like** comfortable?
4 This **tastes** / **tastes like** chicken. What is it?
5 He doesn't **look** / **look like** a doctor.
6 It **feels** / **feels like** colder today.
7 You **look** / **look like** sad. Are you OK?
8 This perfume **smells** / **smells like** flowers.

9 ▶ 7.2 Match 1–4 with a–e. Listen and check. Then act the mini-dialogues with a partner.

▶ Is this glass? _e_
1 Is this strawberry ice cream? ___
2 What's that music? Is it Mozart? ___
3 Is this T-shirt green or brown? ___
4 What's that animal? Is it a rabbit? ___

a It looks brown.
b It looks like a mouse.
c It sounds like Beethoven.
d It tastes like raspberry.
e It feels like plastic.

36   Verbs of sensation

10 GAME Work in small groups. Look at the pictures in exercise 11 and answer the questions. Who can finish first?

In which picture can you see …
- ▶ a person standing behind a tree?   c
1. a person that looks like a cat?   ___
2. a thing that looks like a very big ball?   ___
3. a thing that looks like a kite?   ___
4. a person taking a photo?   ___
5. a person cutting paper?   ___

11 ▶ 7.3 Listen and number the pictures 1–5.

a   b   c ▶   d   e   f

12 Complete the questionnaire, then talk about your answers in small groups. Use *looks* and *sounds*.

What kind of person are you?

How do you feel about these activities?
Rate each activity 1–6.
Use the key below.

paragliding ___	trainspotting ___
zorbing ___	kirigami ___
free running ___	paintballing ___

Key

6 = amazing   3 = OK
5 = exciting   2 = boring
4 = fun   1 = scary

Paintballing sounds fun.

I think it sounds scary.

Self-evaluation Rate your progress.

1
2
3
4
5
6
7
8
9
10
11
12

Unit 7 37

Revision 2   Units 5–7

Reading and writing

1 Look and read. Choose the correct words and write them on the lines.

> cakes   ~~water~~   ice   medicine   onions   sugar

▶ It makes things wet. _water_

1. They are made of flour, eggs, sugar and butter. They taste good. _____
2. This makes food sweet. _____
3. They are vegetables. They make people cry. _____
4. You put it in a drink and it makes the drink cold. _____
5. It makes ill people well again. It often tastes bad. _____

2 Look and read. Write *yes* or *no*.

Let's go home.

▶ The boy's hat looks like a crown. _yes_
1. The cat's made of snow. _____
2. You can see people skiing. _____
3. The boy looks angry. _____
4. The girl in the green jacket looks warm. _____
5. The girl in the green jacket wants to go home. _____

3 Complete the email with the correct form of the verbs in brackets.

Dear Martin

Thanks for your email. The picture made me _laugh_ (laugh)! Do you like ¹_____ (watch) motor sport? I've won two tickets for an event on Saturday 17th. I love ²_____ (go) to things like that, but I don't want ³_____ (go) on my own. Come with me!

I saw you ⁴_____ (talk) to Mr Barnes this morning. He ⁵_____ (seem) angry. Is everything OK?

Best wishes
Jack

4 Read the letter and write the missing words. Write one word on each line.

Dear Claire

Your concert last week was fantastic. It was wonderful to hear _you_ singing again. It made ¹_____ so happy! I wanted ²_____ tell everyone, 'I know her! She's my friend!' You sounded ³_____ a professional singer and you looked fantastic too. Was your dress made ⁴_____ wool?

School holidays start next week. ⁵_____ you like to meet up sometime for a chat?

Mary

38   Units 5–7

Listening

5 ▶ **R4.1** Listen and write.

FITNESS CLUB APPLICATION
PERSONAL PROFILE

Name Nathan Hardy
▶ **Application period** _three_ months
1 **Goals** lose weight; get _____
2 **Likes** _____ and cycling
3 **Why?** likes being _____
4 **Dislikes** skiing and _____
5 **Why?** doesn't like getting _____

6 ▶ **R4.2** What are the objects at the exhibition made of? Listen and write a letter in each box.

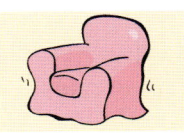

▶ hat b 
1 shoes ☐
2 armchair ☐
3 microwave oven ☐
4 boxing glove ☐
5 handkerchiefs ☐

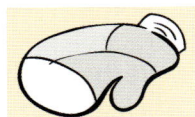

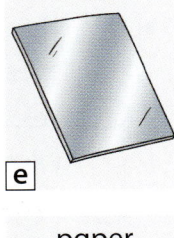

a jelly
b wood
c ice
d glass
e metal
f paper

Speaking

7 Look at the pictures and tell the story.

There are fireworks in the sky. One looks like a flower ...

8 Ask and answer the questions with a partner.

What can you see?
What can you hear?
What makes you laugh?
What makes you scared?
What do you like doing?
What would you like to do next year?

What can you hear?

I can hear people talking and birds singing.

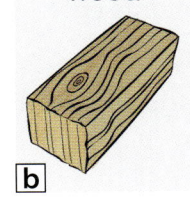

Revision 2   39

8 Present simple and continuous

I can use the present simple to talk about facts and regular events; I can use the present continuous to talk about things happening now, and future arrangements.

Present simple

We use the present simple to talk about regular events and permanent situations.

*Lemons **contain** a lot of vitamin C.*
(fact, permanent situation)
*I **eat** one every day.*
(regular event)

> Why **are** you **eating** a lemon?
> No, thanks!
> Lemons **contain** a lot of vitamin C. I **eat** one every day. **Do** you **want** one?

We form the present simple like this:

Affirmative	Negative	Questions
I / we / you / they **walk** he / she / it **walks**	I / we / you / they **don't walk** (do not walk) he / she / it **doesn't walk** (does not walk)	**Do** I / we / you / they **walk**? **Does** he / she / it **walk**?

Have got means **have**. Notice how questions are formed. We use it to talk about possessions and appearance.
*They**'ve got** a big house.*
***Has** the town **got** a swimming pool?*
~~*Does the town have got a swimming pool?*~~

In English the verbs **like**, **want**, **need**, **know**, and **understand** are always facts, not regular events.
We always use these verbs in the present simple form.
Do you want one? ~~*Are you wanting one?*~~

We often use adverbs of frequency like **never**, **sometimes**, **often**, **always**, **every day / week / year** and **on Fridays** with the present simple.

We form present simple verbs like this:

Most verbs	Verbs ending in -ch, -o, -sh, or -ss	Verbs ending in consonant + -y
+ -s	+ -es	+ -ies
sit → sits walk → walks	watch → watches go → goes	study → studies cry → cries

---

*1 **Circle the correct answer.**
► She **drink** / (**drinks**) milk.
1 We always **have** / **has** breakfast at half past seven.
2 The film **finish** / **finishes** at nine o'clock.
3 He doesn't **like** / **likes** chocolate.
4 Penguins **live** / **lives** in Antarctica.
5 I **don't** / **doesn't** understand.
6 Ben **go** / **goes** swimming every day.
7 Does Andy **live** / **lives** here?
8 Nina and Eric **play** / **plays** tennis at the weekend.
9 **Do** / **Does** you want a sandwich?
10 **Do you** / **Have you** got a phone?

2 Complete the sentences with *do*, *does*, *don't* or *doesn't*.
► ○ <u>Do</u> you do your homework every night?
   ○ Yes, I <u>do</u>.
1 ○ What <u>does</u> this word mean?
   ○ I <u>don't</u> know. Sorry.
2 ○ What <u>does</u> elephants eat?
   ○ Fruit, vegetables, and nuts.
3 ○ <u>Does</u> your sister go to school?
   ○ No, she <u>doesn't</u>.

40 Present simple and continuous

3 Complete the sentences with the present simple form of the verbs in brackets. Then match a–g with 1–6.

▶ She's a photographer. She _takes_ (take) photos of the band. _f_
1 He's a cook. He _MAKES_ (make) their breakfast, lunch and dinner. _E_
2 He's a singer. He _SINGING_ (sing) in their music videos. _G_
3 He's a fan. He _HAS_ (have) all their songs and he _GOES_ (go) to all their concerts. _C_
4 She's a fan. She _LOVES_ (love) all their music and she _BUYS_ (buy) all their songs. _D_
5 He's a pilot. He _FLYES_ (fly) the band around the world. _A_
6 She's a hairdresser. She _WASHES_ (wash) and _BRUSHES_ (brush) their hair. _B_

4 GAME Work in pairs. Look at the picture in exercise 3. Cover the sentences. Talk about the people and their jobs. How much can you remember?

Who's she?

She's a photographer. She takes photos of the band.

5 Write the questions and your short answers.

▶ you / speak Spanish?
Do you speak Spanish? No, I don't.
1 you / study at the weekend?
DO YOU STUDY AT THE WEEKEND? YES, I DO
2 your friends / like football?
DO YOUR FRIEND LIKE FOTABALL? YES, they DO
3 you and your best friend / talk every day?
Do you talk every day? No, I don't
4 you / watch European and American films?
DO YOU WATCH European and American? yes, I DO
5 you / fly a kite on windy days?
No, I don't
6 your friends / play computer games?
DO YOUR friends play computer games? yes, they do.

6 ▶ 8.1 Listen to Martin. Choose the correct answers.

▶ Martin **speaks** / (**doesn't speak**) Spanish.
1 Martin's friends **play** / **don't play** football.
2 Martin and his best friend **talk** / **don't talk** every day.
3 Martin **watches** / **doesn't watch** English and American films.
4 Martin **flies** / **doesn't fly** a kite on windy days.
5 Martin's best friend **plays** / **doesn't play** computer games.

7 Use the questions in exercise 5 to interview your partner.

James, do you speak Spanish?

No, I don't.

Do your friends eat meat?

Yes, they do.

Unit 8   41

Present continuous

We use the present continuous to talk about things happening now:

He's reading my newspaper!

We also use the present continuous to talk about things happening around now. These are temporary situations:

She's reading a lot of books at the moment.

We form the present continuous like this:

Affirmative	Negative	Questions
I'm walking we / you / they're walking he / she / it's walking	I'm not walking we / you / they aren't walking he / she / it isn't walking	Am I walking? Are we / you / they walking? Is he / she / it walking?

Heidi's wearing a red dress.
We're having lunch.

I'm not thinking about it this week.
It isn't raining at the moment.

Is Sam coming?
Where are you going?

Present continuous verbs change like this:

Most verbs	Verbs ending -e	Verbs ending vowel + consonant
+ -ing	remove -e, + -ing	double the final consonant, + -ing
sing → singing look → looking	write → writing smile → smiling	sit → sitting put → putting

We use the present continuous to talk about future plans and arrangements with other people.
I'm having lunch at school tomorrow.
Jack's playing tennis with Ed on Friday.

We often use these time expressions with the present continuous for now or around now:
now, this week, today, at the moment

We use these time expressions with the present continuous for future arrangements:
tomorrow, next Friday, on Tuesday, this evening

---

*8 ▶ **8.2** Who is who? Listen and write the names.

Max   Rosy   ~~Louise~~   Tim   Beth
Edward   Alice   Ted   Henry

▶ _Louise_ is Rosy's cousin.
1 _____ is Louise's husband.
2 _____ and _____ are playing 'Scissors Paper Stone'.
3 _____ is throwing rice.
4 Rosy's grandma, _____, is crying.
5 _____ is filming the wedding.
6 _____ is holding the flowers.

9 **GAME Work in groups. Choose one of the activities. Act it. Can the others guess what you're doing?

make a sandwich   fly a kite   walk the dog
play tennis   swim   do your homework
read a newspaper   make a phone call

What am I doing?

Are you swimming?

Yes, I am.

42   Present simple and continuous

10 Look at the diaries. Complete the sentences with the verbs in brackets.

Carrie's diary
Sunday — Write songs with Angie B
Monday — Go shopping with Louise
Tuesday — 2 p.m. – meet new manager
Wednesday — Free day!!
Thursday — Children's hospital visit

The band's diary
Thursday — 11 a.m. Children's hospital visit
Friday — Talk on a TV show
Saturday — Concert in Paris
Sunday — Fly to New York

▶ On Sunday Carrie _'s writing_ (write) songs with Angie B.
1 She _____ (go) shopping with Louise on Monday.
2 She _____ (meet) a new manager at 2 p.m. on Tuesday.
3 She _____ (not do) anything on Wednesday.
4 Carrie and the band _____ (visit) a children's hospital at 11 o'clock on Thursday morning.
5 They _____ (give) a concert in Paris on Saturday.
6 They _____ (fly) to New York on Sunday.

11 Work in pairs.

Student A
You're Carrie. Look at the diary and answer your partner's questions. Use *I* and *we*.

Student B
You're a music journalist. Ask Carrie about her and the band's plans and arrangements.

> What are you doing on Tuesday?

> I'm writing songs with Angie B.

12 Circle the present simple or present continuous to complete each conversation.

▶ Hey! Where **do you go** / (**are you going**)?
  To the park. I **meet** / (**'m meeting**) Alex for a game of tennis.
1 **Does Mary go** / **Is Mary going** to Art Club on Wednesdays?
  I **don't know** / **'m not knowing**.
2 Why **do you walk** / **are you walking** to school today?
  Because my brother **uses** / **'s using** my bike this week.
3 We **have** / **'re having** a barbecue on Saturday afternoon. **Do you want** / **Are you wanting** to come?
  Thanks, but we **go** / **'re going** to my grandparents' house every Saturday.

13 **GAME** Work in pairs. Can you find ten more differences?

> In picture 1 the girl is writing a letter but in picture 2 she's drawing a picture.

Picture 1

Picture 2

Unit 8 43

14 ▶ 8.3 Listen to two people playing 'Who am I?' Which pictures do they choose?

Person 1 _____   Person 2 _____

15 GAME Work in pairs. Student A: Choose a picture from exercise 14 and keep it a secret.
Student B: Ask five *yes/no* questions. Can you guess which picture student A is thinking of?

Are you a boy?
Yes, I am.

Are you running?
No, I'm not.

Is the sun shining?
Yes, it is.

44 Present simple and continuous

16 Complete the email with the present simple or present continuous form of the verb in brackets.

Hello!

I'm writing (write) to you from my tent. It's our annual family summer holiday – and the weather's terrible! Right now, it ¹_____ (rain) and the wind ²_____ (blow). It feels like winter. What's the weather like with you today?

We ³_____ (stay) in a field near the mountains. We ⁴_____ (come) here every year. I ⁵_____ (not know) why. I really ⁶_____ (not like) camping. My things always ⁷_____ (get) wet and dirty. I ⁸_____ (want) to stay in a big hotel by the sea in a hot country!

What about you? ⁹_____ (you / like) camping? ¹⁰_____ (you / have) a holiday every year? Where ¹¹_____ (you / go)?

I hope the rain stops soon. This afternoon we ¹²_____ (take) a boat out on the lake.

See you soon.
Toby
P.S. I ¹³_____ (come) home at the weekend. How about you? ¹⁴_____ (you / have) any plans for the weekend?

17 Write to Toby. Answer his questions. Tell him about the weather today, your typical family holiday, and your plans for today and tomorrow.

Hi Toby
Thanks for your letter. I'm at home with my family.

18 Use the prompts to make true sentences. Use the present simple + *always*, *never*, *sometimes*, or the present continuous + *today* or *at the moment*.

▶ I / wear / pink socks
I never wear pink socks.

1 I / use / a blue pen
_____

2 I / feel / hungry
_____

3 I / wear / trainers
_____

4 I / read / science fiction
_____

5 I / wear / glasses
_____

6 I / want / lots of homework
_____

7 I / sit / by the door
_____

8 My English / get / better
_____

Self-evaluation Rate your progress.

Unit 8   45

9 Past simple

I can recognize and use the past simple to talk about past events.

Was, were

We use the past simple for actions, events and situations that happened at a definite time in the past. We often use past time expressions with the past simple.

yesterday, yesterday morning, yesterday afternoon, last night, last week, in September, two days ago, in 1988

For more information on past time expressions, see Unit 22.

Did you see the fireworks last night? They were brilliant!

No, I didn't. I was asleep in bed.

But they started at seven o'clock!

I went to bed early. I was tired. Were they noisy?

Yes, they were.

Oh. Well, I didn't wake up.

The past simple of **be** has two forms: **was** and **were**.

Affirmative	Negative	Question
I / he / she / it **was** we / you / they **were**	I / he / she / it **wasn't** we / you / they **weren't**	**Was** I / he / she / it …? **Were** we / you / they …?

I **was** here.
You **were** right.

It **wasn't** difficult.
They **weren't** late.

Were you OK? Yes, I **was**.
Was he in the garden? No, he **wasn't**.

***1 Circle the correct answer.**

▶ They **was** / (**were**) here yesterday.
1 Where **was** / **were** you?
2 The film **was** / **were** funny.
3 What **was** / **were** the weather like?
4 We **wasn't** / **weren't** hungry.
5 **Was** / **Were** Jill at school?
6 He **wasn't** / **weren't** a doctor.
7 **Was** / **Were** Leo and Sam there?
8 You **wasn't** / **weren't** at the cinema.

**2 Write questions with *was* and *were* and short answers with *was*, *were*, *was* and *wasn't*.

▶ you / at school
<u>Were you at school</u> yesterday?
<u>No, I wasn't.</u>

1 it / cold
_____ yesterday?
_____

2 your friends / happy
_____ yesterday?
_____

3 you / tired
_____ last night?
_____

46 Past simple

Past simple: regular verbs

We form the past simple of regular verbs by adding -**ed** to the verb.
play → play**ed**   ask → ask**ed**   start → start**ed**   wash → wash**ed**
I **cleaned** my room yesterday.   They **waited** for two hours.
Look at these other regular spelling rules:

Add -**d** to verbs ending in -**e**.	Change -**y** to -**ied** in verbs ending in consonant + -**y**.
like → lik**ed** share → shar**ed**	study → stud**ied** cry → cr**ied**

Double the last letter and then add -ed to most verbs ending in one vowel and one consonant.
travel → trave**lled**   chat → cha**tted**

We use **did** or **didn't** and the base form for questions and negative forms.
I **didn't enjoy** the film.   When **did** you **start** that book?

*3 Write the verbs in the past simple.

▶ visit _visited_   5 plan _____
1 rain _____   6 miss _____
2 tidy _____   7 drop _____
3 call _____   8 cook _____
4 try _____   9 receive _____

*4 ▶ 9.1 Listen and repeat.

/d/: climbed, stayed, enjoyed
/t/: jumped, walked, watched
/ɪd/: wanted, ended, landed

**5 Complete the affirmative and negative past simple sentences and questions.

▶ I usually play tennis.
   (+) Yesterday, I _played_ football.
1 We usually chat online.
   (–) Yesterday, we _____ on the phone.
2 Do you like the food today?
   (?) _____ the food yesterday?
3 He lives in this house now.
   (+) He _____ in this house 5 years ago.
4 My sister doesn't want to go.
   (–) She _____ to go last week.
5 Does it work now?
   (?) _____ yesterday?
6 I study Japanese.
   (+) My aunt _____ Japanese in 1974.

***6 GAME ▶ 9.2 Write the verbs in brackets in the past simple, then match 1–7 with a–h. You can look on the internet for help. Listen and check your answers.

▶ _acted_   (act) in films. _g_
1 _____   (compose) music. ___
2 _____   (play) tennis. ___
3 _____   (paint) pictures. ___
4 _____   (live) from 1935 to 1977. ___
5 _____   (die) in 2009. ___
6 _____   (invent) the X-ray machine. ___
7 _____   (study) stars and planets. ___

a Billie Jean King
b Elvis Presley
c Pyotr Tchaikovsky
d Marie Curie
e Galileo Galilei
f Vincent Van Gogh
g ~~Cary Grant~~
h Michael Jackson

Unit 9   47

7 Complete the magazine article with the past simple form of the verb in brackets.

Two Young Adventurers Solo Round-the-World Sailors

Michael Perham and Jessica Watson are the World's two youngest round-the-world sailors. Michael _was_ (be) born in the UK in 1992. When he was 17 he ¹_____ (sail) around the world alone. At the time he ²_____ (be) the youngest person to do this.

Michael ³_____ (start) his journey in November 2008 and ⁴_____ (finish) it in August 2009. He originally ⁵_____ (want) to do the journey in four months without any help.

In the end, this ⁶_____ (not / be) possible because of problems with his boat.

There ⁷_____ (be) also problems with the weather. He ⁸_____ (not / sail) around Cape Horn because there ⁹_____ (be) bad storms in the Southern Ocean. Instead he ¹⁰_____ (sail) through the Panama Canal.

Jessica ¹¹_____ (be) born in Australia in 1993. When she was a child she had sailing lessons. For five years she and her family ¹²_____ (not / live) in a house or flat: they ¹³_____ (live) on a boat at sea.

In 2010 she ¹⁴_____ (complete) her first solo round-the-world sailing trip – at the age of just 16. She ¹⁵_____ (not / receive) any help on her trip.

8 Work in pairs. Cover the article in exercise 7. Look at the pictures below and write J (Jessica) or M (Michael). Make sentences in the past simple with your partner.

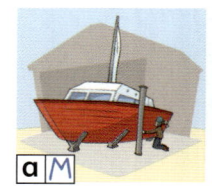

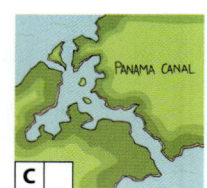

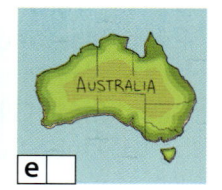

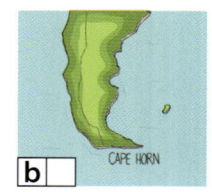

a [M] c [ ] e [ ]
b [ ] d [ ] f [ ]

(Jessica had problems with her boat.)
(No, Michael had problems with his boat.)

9 Complete the questions with *was*, *were* or *did*.

▶ What _did_ you watch on TV yesterday?
1 How _____ your weekend?
2 Where _____ you live in 2008?
3 _____ you study for any exams last month?
4 Where _____ you at four o'clock yesterday afternoon?
5 _____ a friend phone you yesterday?
6 Where _____ you born?
7 What _____ the weather like yesterday?
8 When _____ you start learning English?

10 Use the questions in exercise 10 to interview a partner.

(What did you watch on TV yesterday?)
(I watched a film.)

Past simple

Past simple: irregular verbs

Many verbs have an irregular past simple form.
come → **came**   say → **said**
do → **did**   see → **saw**
fall → **fell**   sit → **sat**
find → **found**   sing → **sang**
go → **went**   sleep → **slept**
have → **had**   take → **took**
put → **put**   think → **thought**
ring → **rang**   win → **won**

We **went** to the shops.   I **bought** some books.

For a longer list of irregular verbs, see page 160.

We use **did** or **didn't** + base form for questions and negative forms.
He **didn't say** that!   Where **did** you **get** that pen?

*11 ▶ 9.3 Look at the list of irregular verbs on page 160. Write the past simple forms of these verbs. Then listen and repeat.

▶ give	_gave_	10 hit	_____
1 leave	_____	11 meet	_____
2 swim	_____	12 eat	_____
3 lie	_____	13 lose	_____
4 run	_____	14 sleep	_____
5 read	_____	15 write	_____
6 sit	_____	16 spend	_____
7 drink	_____	17 get	_____
8 hurt	_____	18 begin	_____
9 make	_____	19 say	_____

**12 Complete the table with the base form of the verbs. Look at the list of irregular verbs on page 160.

▶ _come_	came	5 _____	sang
▶ _become_	became	6 _____	rang
1 _____	slept	7 _____	told
2 _____	kept	8 _____	sold
3 _____	thought	9 _____	taught
4 _____	brought	10 _____	caught

*13 Complete the email with the past simple form of the verb in brackets.

Dear Grandpa
How are you? I _rang_ (ring) you yesterday but Grandma said you were in the garden.
Guess what? Tommy ¹_____ (come) to our house yesterday. He ²_____ (bring) a fish with him! He ³_____ (say), 'I ⁴_____ (catch) it in the river.'
Mum cooked the fish and Dad ⁵_____ (make) a salad. We ⁶_____ (sit) and ⁷_____ (eat) in the garden. We all ⁸_____ (have) a fantastic evening.
See you soon.
John

**14 ▶ 9.4 Complete the conversations. Then listen and check. Act the conversations with a partner.

▶ 💬 Did you drink my juice?
  💬 No, I _drank_ my juice!
1 💬 Did you sleep in a tent?
  💬 No, we _____ on the beach!
2 💬 _____ a newspaper?
  💬 No, I got a magazine.
3 💬 Did you meet Julie?
  💬 No, I _____ Jenny.
4 💬 _____ any birds?
  💬 No, but I saw some butterflies.
5 💬 Did you have lunch?
  💬 Yes, I _____ a sandwich.

Unit 9   49

15 ▶ 9.5 Work in pairs. Look at the picture story. Put the pictures in order 1–6. Then listen and check.

16 ▶ 9.5 Circle the correct answers. Then listen again and check.

▶ It **was** / **wasn't** warm in the morning.
1 Rosy **rang** / **met** Sophia at lunchtime.
2 They **ate their picnic** / **spent some time** in the forest.
3 They **listened to** / **sang** music **in the forest** / **in the field**.
4 They **took** / **didn't take** two MP3 players with them.
5 They **went** / **didn't go** under a tree when the lightning started.
6 Sophia **put** / **didn't put** her MP3 player headphones in her pocket.
7 The lightning **hurt** / **didn't hurt** Rosy and Sophia a little.
8 The MP3 player **was** / **wasn't** OK.

17 Work in two groups. Write past tense questions for the answers. Use the prompts.

▶ what / weather / be / like?
<u>What was the weather like?</u>
It was warm and sunny.
1 (where / Sophia and Rosy / go first?)
_____
They went to the forest.
2 (where / they / sit / in the storm?)
_____
They sat on the grass.
3 (where / Sophia and Rosy / have / a picnic?)
_____
They had a picnic in a field.
4 (where / put / hands / in the storm?)
_____
They put their hands on their heads.
5 (who / the lightning / hit?)
_____
The lightning hit Sophia and Rosy.
6 (how / they / feel?)
_____
They felt frightened.
7 (where / be / the MP3 player?)
_____
It was in Sophia's pocket.
8 (where / go / after the storm)
_____
They went to hospital.

18 Work in pairs. Tell the story of Sophia and Rosy. Use these verbs.

listen begin be go take have start
ring meet sit put hit find

It was a warm and sunny morning. Rosy rang Sophia and they …

50 Past simple

19 🎵 ▶ 9.6 Read and listen. Then listen again and complete the song with the verbs below in the past simple. Match each part of the song to a picture. Listen again and repeat.

walk   sit   eat   ~~spend~~   jump   enjoy   stay   read   run   be

1
How was your summer?
Did you have a good break?
How did you spend each day?
I <u>spent</u> each day
with a group of friends.
We climbed, we ¹_____,
we ²_____, we swam.
We chatted, we ³_____,
we stayed up late.
We ⁴_____ happy each day …

2
How was your summer?
Did you have a good break?
How did you spend each day?
I didn't do much.
I ⁵_____ at home.
I didn't go travelling
to Shanghai or Rome.
I dreamt, I ⁶_____.
I lay on my bed.
I ⁷_____ happy each day …

3
How was your summer?
Did you have a good break?
How did you spend each day?
I ⁸_____ out of the house
from morning till night.
I ⁹_____ the fresh air.
The world felt right.
I ¹⁰_____ in the fields.
I ¹¹_____ by a tree.
I ¹²_____ happy each day …

20 ✏️ 💬 Underline five things in the song that you did on your last holiday. Circle five things that you didn't do. Write sentences. Then compare your sentences in groups.

On my last holiday I chatted with my friends and I stayed up late.
I didn't walk in the fields.

Unit 9   51

21 GAME Work in large groups. Ask questions to find the information below. When a classmate says 'yes' write his or her name. The first person with six names is the winner.

Find someone who...
... had hot food for breakfast. Sam
... didn't spend any money yesterday. _____
... sang a song yesterday. _____
... chatted online at the weekend. _____
... swam in the sea last year. _____
... walked in the woods or by the sea last weekend. _____
... didn't stay up late last night. _____
... travelled to another country last year. _____
... tidied his or her bedroom yesterday. _____
... was born in January, June or July. _____

Did you have hot food for breakfast, Kate?

No, I didn't.

Did you have hot food for breakfast, Sam?

Yes, I did. I had eggs.

22 Answer the questions below.

What did you do on your last birthday?

On my last birthday I got up late and I had pancakes for breakfast.

What did you do last weekend?

What did you do on your last holiday?

Self-evaluation Rate your progress.

52   Past simple

10 Past continuous

I can recognize and use the past continuous to give background information and to talk about interrupted past events.

It was a dark evening. Max Butler **was walking** down a dark, narrow street. The wind **was blowing** and it **was raining**. Suddenly, Max heard a noise behind him. He stopped and turned round.

We use the past continuous to talk about situations in progress at a time in the past. We often use the past continuous in stories.

past ←————×————————→ now

8.30, running, singing
At half past eight this morning I **was running** to school. The birds **were singing**.

We form the past continuous like this.

Affirmative	Negative
I / he / she / it **was running**	I / he / she / it **wasn't running**
we / you / they **were running**	we / you / they **weren't running**

Pete **was working**.   James and Anna **were talking**.   I **wasn't crying**.   You **weren't looking**.

Questions		
Was I / he / she / it **running**?	**Were** we / you / they **running**?	Yes, we **were**. No, they **weren't**.

Was the sun **shining**? Yes, it **was**.   **Were** Bella and Henry **eating**? No, they **weren't**.

*1 ▶ 10.1 Listen and circle the correct answer.
▶ He was playing the **guitar** / (**drums**).
1 The babies were **crying** / **laughing**.
2 It **was** / **wasn't** raining.
3 She was **running** / **walking**.
4 They were **laughing** / **shouting**.
5 The birds **were** / **weren't** singing.
6 He was **listening to music** / **playing a musical instrument**.
7 They were playing **tennis** / **basketball**.
8 She was riding **a bike** / **a horse**.
9 He was cleaning **his teeth** / **the floor**.

**2 Work in pairs. Ask and answer questions about exercise 1.

Was he playing the guitar?
No, he wasn't. He was playing the drums.
Were the babies crying?
Yes, they were.

3 ▶ **10.2** Read the poem and complete it with the verbs from the box. Listen and check, then listen and repeat.

are doing thinking feeling ~~doing~~ sleeping looking were weren't wasn't wearing

What were you doing yesterday?
We didn't see you at school.
We were ¹_____ about you yesterday.
We didn't see you at all.

Yesterday, I was feeling ill.
I was ²_____ and resting all day.
I was ³_____ pyjamas at lunchtime,
My face was tired and grey.

What were you ⁴_____ yesterday?
We didn't see you at school.
We ⁵_____ talking about you yesterday.
We didn't see you at all.

I ⁶_____ feeling well at all,
I was ⁷_____ really bad.
I was lying in bed and ⁸_____ at books,
I was feeling really sad.

I'm sorry you ⁹_____ feeling well.
How ¹⁰_____ you feeling today?
I'm feeling much, much better, thanks –
Come on, let's go and play!

4 Complete the sentences with the past continuous form of the verbs in brackets.

▶ She _was writing_ (write) an email.
1 You _____ (sleep)!
2 We _____ (have) some problems with the computer this morning.
3 I _____ (dream) about a flying fish.
4 It _____ (snow) last night.
5 They _____ (not / help) us.
6 The phone _____ (not / work) yesterday.
7 You _____ (not / listen) to me.
8 She _____ (watch) a film at seven o'clock.
9 Where _____ (they / go)?
10 _____ (it / rain) at six o'clock?
11 _____ (you / wearing) jeans yesterday?
12 Why _____ (he / not / look) at it?

5 ▶ **10.3** Listen again and complete the pronunciation information. Then practise reading the poem in exercise 3 with a partner.

1 We **stress** / **don't stress** *was* and *were* in the poem.
2 We **stress** / **don't stress** *was* and *wasn't* in the poem.

6 Complete the questions with the past continuous form of the verb in brackets.

▶ What _were you doing_ (you / do) yesterday?
1 How _____ (you / feel) yesterday?
2 What _____ (you / wear) yesterday?
3 What English grammar _____ (you / study) last week?

7 Work in pairs. Ask and answer the questions in exercise 6.

What were you doing yesterday?
I was studying at school.

54 Past continuous

8 **GAME** Work in pairs. Look at the pictures. Can you find ten differences? Use the past continuous.

At seven o'clock in the morning …

At seven o'clock in the evening …

At seven o'clock in the morning the girl was wearing her school uniform, but at seven o'clock in the evening she wasn't wearing her school uniform.

In the morning the boy …

9 **GAME** Work in pairs or small groups. Look at the picture on page 154 for two minutes. How many questions can you answer together?

▶ What was the tour guide pointing at?
  He was pointing at a statue.
1 What was the man taking a photo of?
  _____
2 What were the children eating?
  _____
3 What was the boy holding?
  _____
4 What colour sunglasses was the woman wearing?
  _____
5 What was the bird doing?
  _____
6 What was the weather like?
  _____
7 What was the man reading?
  _____
8 What were the two performers doing?
  _____

10 Make questions from the prompts. Then use the questions to interview a partner.

▶ What / you / do at ten o'clock yesterday morning?
1 Where / you / live in 2004?
2 What / you / do at six o'clock this morning?
3 What / you / do at five o'clock yesterday afternoon?
4 What / you / wear last Saturday?
5 the sun / shine yesterday morning?
6 What colour socks / you / wear yesterday?

What were you doing at ten o'clock yesterday morning?

It was a sports lesson. I was running.

Unit 10   55

Past continuous and past simple

We often use the past continuous with the past simple, especially when we tell stories.

We use the past simple to talk about a completed past event.

*The phone **rang**.*

To talk about two events that happened at the same time we use the past continuous and the past simple.

*The phone **rang**. We **were watching** a film.*

We can link these sentences with **when**.

When	Past simple	Past continuous
When	the phone **rang**	we **were watching** a film.

Past simple	when	Past continuous
The phone **rang**	when	we **were watching** a film.

Past continuous	when	Past simple
We **were watching** a film	when	the phone **rang**.

We can use two verbs in the **past continuous** with **and** to talk about two past actions in progress at the same time.
*I **was doing** my homework **and** my grandma **was making** soup.*

56 Past continuous

*11 ▶ 10.4 Listen and match a–h and 1–8.

*12 **GAME** Work in pairs. Look at pictures 1–8 in exercise 11. Cover pictures a–h. How many sentences can you remember?

The phone rang when we were eating dinner.

It was raining when …

**13 Circle the correct answers.
▶ When I (**looked**) / **was looking** out of the window it **snowed** / (**was snowing**)
1 We **worked** / **were working** in the garden when we **found** / **were finding** some old money.
2 When I **made** / **was making** the cake I **dropped** / **was dropping** the bowl.
3 I **cleaned** / **was cleaning** the kitchen when she **arrived** / **was arriving**.
4 When I **started** / **was starting** school we **lived** / **were living** in the old house.
5 I **saw** / **was seeing** you when I **waited** / **was waiting** for the bus.

14 **GAME** Work in pairs. Combine different pictures from exercise 8 to make past continuous sentences. How many can you make?

He hurt his head when he was skiing.

The sun was shining when we were playing football.

15 ▶ 10.5 Work in pairs. Look at the pictures. Try to put the pictures in order from 1–8. Then listen and check.

a
b 1
c
d
e
f
g
h

16 Match the rules.
When we tell a story we use
1 The **past simple** for ___.
2 The **past continuous** for ___.
a background information
b the main events and actions

17 ▶ 10.5 Complete the text with the past simple or past continuous form of the verbs in brackets. Then listen again and check.

This <u>happened</u> (happen) last week when I was in the park. The sun ¹_____ (shine) and I ²_____ (sit) on the grass. I ³_____ (paint) a picture of the ducks on the pond.

Some children ⁴_____ (play) football. Suddenly, their ball ⁵_____ (hit) my paint pots and the paint pots ⁶_____ (fall) over. The blue paint went on my picture and the pink paint ⁷_____ (go) on the grass.

My hands got dirty when I ⁸_____ (clean) my picture so I decided to go and wash them in the pond. The ducks ⁹_____ (fly) away when I ¹⁰_____ (wash) my hands because they were scared of me.

They ¹¹_____ (land) on the grass by my picture. They walked on the pink paint, then they ¹²_____ (walk) on my picture. They ¹³_____ (make) pink marks all over the paper.

And that wasn't all. When the ducks ¹⁴_____ (walk) on my picture it ¹⁵_____ (start) to rain. By now my picture looked terrible.
I ¹⁶_____ (think) about what to do with the picture when a girl ¹⁷_____ (speak) to me.

'I love your picture,' she ¹⁸_____ (say). So what did I do? I gave it to her!

Unit 10   57

18 Look at the pictures. Write a story called 'Tom's Hat'. Use the past continuous and the past simple with the verbs in the box.

walk   wear   sit   stand   snow   get on the bus
get off the bus   put   give   fall   pull   find
see   talk   give

TOM'S HAT

Tom was walking to school. It was snowing. He was wearing a hat, a scarf and gloves.

He got on the bus and he …

19 How does 'Tom's Hat' end? Write the end of the story.

Tom walked into the park. He …

20 Work in pairs. Read your ending of 'Tom's Hat' to your partner. Which ending do you like best?

OK, here's my ending. When Tom was walking into the park he saw …

Self-evaluation Rate your progress.

	😊	😊😊	😊😊😊
1			
2			
3			
4			
5			
6			
7			
8			
9			
10			
11			
12			
13			
14			
15			
16			
17			
18			
19			
20			

Mini-revision Units 8–10

Reading and writing

1 Read the story. Choose a word from the box. Write the correct word next to numbers 1–5.

> couldn't do didn't don't
> doesn't isn't 're ~~'ve~~ was were

I **'ve** got a cousin called Sam. We often do sports together. We meet at the weekend because he ¹_____ go to the same school as me.
At the moment we ²_____ playing a lot of tennis because it's summer.

I always wear a blue cap for tennis. Sam wears a red cap. Yesterday I looked everywhere for my blue cap, but I ³_____ find it.

When I arrived at the park, Sam ⁴_____ wearing his red cap – and my blue cap! 'You left it here last week,' he explained. 'So I put it with mine. I ⁵_____ want to forget it.'

2 Read the story. Write the correct form of the verbs in brackets.

A few months ago, George and his friends were **cycling** (cycle) in the hills when they heard a strange noise. George's friends ¹_____ (not stop) cycling, but George stopped and got off his bike.

He looked around but he couldn't ²_____ (see) anything. The noise stopped. Then George looked down and ³_____ (see) something white at his feet. It ⁴_____ (be) an envelope.

He picked it up and opened it. He couldn't believe his eyes. There was £10,000 inside! George took the money to the police. Will someone ask for it? George is still ⁵_____ (wait) to hear.

Listening

3 ▶ R5.1 Listen and draw lines.

Alex   Milly   Vicky   Sarah

Jason   Jimmy   Ben

Speaking

4 Work with a partner. Ask and answer the questions together.

▶ What / the teacher / do / at the moment?
1 the sun / shine at the moment?
2 What / you / do / at five o'clock this morning?
3 What / you / have / for breakfast today?
4 you / think about school / at the weekend?
5 you / watch TV yesterday?
6 your English / get better?

What's the teacher doing at the moment?

He's writing on the board.

Units 8–10   59

11 Present perfect

I can recognize and use the present perfect to talk about past events, experiences and situations.

Present perfect

We use the present perfect to talk about past events that are connected to the present in some way. We often use it to describe change.
I've lost my glasses.
(= I can't find my glasses.)
She's visited Paris three times.
(= She knows what Paris is like.)

We form the present perfect with the present simple of **have** and the past participle.

Affirmative
I / we / you / they**'ve** (**have**) **started**
he / she / it**'s** (**has**) **started**

Negative
I / we / you / they **haven't started**
he / she / it **hasn't started**

Questions
Have you (I / we) **started**?
Yes, I (we / you / they) **have**.
No, I (we / you / they) **haven't**.
Has he (she / it) **started**?
Yes, he (she / it) **has**.
No, he (she / it) **hasn't**.

I've lost my glasses.

You haven't lost them. They're on your head!

Most verbs have regular past participles. They are formed like regular past simple verbs.
clean → clean**ed**   arrive → arriv**ed**
study → stud**ied**   try → tr**ied**
travel → trave**lled**   stop → sto**pped**
He's changed his name.
Have you ever *tried* skateboarding?

Other verbs have an irregular past participle form. Here are some irregular past participles. For a longer list, look at page 160.
drink → **drunk**   see → **seen**   eat → **eaten**
swim → **swum**   fall → **fallen**   take → **taken**
go → **been**   write → **written**
I've written a letter.
Have you *seen* Andy?

*1 Write the past participles of these regular and irregular verbs.

▶ phone — *phoned*
1 want _____
2 talk _____
3 leave _____
4 cry _____
5 tell _____
6 kick _____
7 work _____
8 chat _____
9 brush _____
10 build _____
11 enjoy _____
12 fix _____
13 plan _____
14 think _____
15 give _____

*2 Write the past simple and past participles of these verbs.

	Past simple	Past participle
▶ know	*knew*	*known*
1 finish		
2 catch		
3 forget		
4 do		
5 put		
6 happen		
7 break		

3 Complete the sentences with the present perfect. Use the verbs in brackets.

▶ She _'s seen_ (see) the photo.
1 Paul _____ (clean) the floor.
2 The flowers _____ (not grow) a lot.
3 I _____ (tell) Ernie about it.
4 She _____ (not do) her homework.
5 We _____ (have) lunch.
6 David _____ (not see) us.
7 We _____ (win)!
8 The film _____ (not start).

4 Write questions and short answers about the pictures. Use the prompts.

▶ close / the door? _Have they closed the door? No, they haven't._

1 pick / some flowers? _____

2 build / a tower? _____

3 win / the match? _____

4 cut / the trees down? _____

5 bring / an umbrella? _____

5 Work in small groups. How many responses with the present perfect can you think of?

1 You look upset.
2 You look happy.
3 You look tired.
4 You look sad.

You look upset.
My bike's disappeared.
I've lost my phone.

6 GAME What's changed? Work in pairs. Use the verbs in the box.

build   burn   change   into   cut down   fix
grow   open   paint   pick   plant   water

Picture 1

Picture 2

The man has cut down the tree.
The bird has built a nest.

Unit 11   61

Present perfect and past simple

We use the present perfect to talk about past events when the exact time of the event is either obvious or not important.
I've finished this book.
Have you **ever ridden** a horse?
I've never eaten sushi.

When the past time is important, we use the past simple and an exact time expression. We also use the past simple when we give extra information about an event.
I finished this book **yesterday**.
Did you **ride** a horse **at the weekend**?
I didn't do that **when I was a child**.

We use **recently** with the present perfect to talk about events in the near past.
Have you **spoken** to Frank **recently**?
I haven't played much basketball **recently**.

Have you stayed in a five-star hotel recently?

Me? I've never stayed in a five-star hotel! But I stayed in a one-star hotel in 2010. It was terrible!

We often use **ever** and **never** with the present perfect when we ask and talk about experiences.
Have you **ever spoken** to Frank?
I've never played basketball.

We can also use these expressions:
once, **twice** (= two times), **lots of times**
I've eaten Japanese food **once**.
He's climbed that mountain **lots of times**.

*7 **Choose the correct time expression.**
▶ You've worked hard (**recently**) / **on Monday**.
1 It snowed **recently** / **in 2010**.
2 Has he **ever** / **recently** taken a photo of you?
3 I haven't eaten any chocolate **yesterday** / **recently**.
4 She's met Helen **in September** / **twice**.
5 We saw Jack **ever** / **at nine o'clock**.
6 They've **never** / **at the weekend** visited us.
7 Did he phone you **recently** / **on Sunday**?
8 I've read this book **never** / **lots of times**.

8 ▶ 11.1 Add the words in brackets to the correct place in the sentence. Then listen, check and repeat.
▶ Has he ˄ever˄ won a prize? (ever)
1 Have you taken a photo of them? (recently)
2 She's had a dog. (never)
3 We've talked a lot. (recently)
4 I've broken my arm. (once)
5 It hasn't rained. (recently)
6 You've told that story. (lots of times)

*9 **What have you or haven't you done recently? Write true sentences with have or haven't + recently.**
▶ play a computer game
   <u>I've played a computer game recently.</u>
1 travel to another town or city
   _____
2 tidy my bedroom
   _____
3 use a dictionary
   _____
4 do my homework
   _____
5 visit my aunts and uncles
   _____
6 help with the housework
   _____
7 watch a film on TV
   _____
8 make a lot of grammar mistakes
   _____

10 What experiences have you or haven't you had? Talk about your experiences.

▶ travel by plane
1 break a bone
2 go to the desert
3 plant a tree
4 see a scorpion
5 catch a fish

I've travelled by plane two or three times.

I've never travelled by plane.

I've travelled by plane lots of times.

11 🔊 11.2 Complete the 'Me' column. Then listen to Dora, Jason and Ivy and complete the table.

✓✓ = Yes, recently.   ✗ = Never.
✓ = Yes, but not recently.

	Me	Dora	Ivy	Jason
climb a mountain		✓✓	✓	✗
stay in a five-star hotel				
camp				
pick fresh fruit				
try snorkelling				
try scuba diving				

12 🔊 11.3 Circle the correct answers to complete part of the conversation. Then listen again and check. Work in groups of three. Act out the conversation.

Ivy   Hi Dora. How are you?
Dora   Good. Thanks, Ivy. **I've had** / I had the most amazing holiday.
Ivy   Lucky you! ¹**What have you done?** / What did you do?
Dora   It was a very active holiday. One day we ²**'ve climbed** / **climbed** right to the top of a mountain.
Jason ³**I've never climbed** / **I never climbed** a mountain. ⁴**I've climbed** / **I climbed** a big hill but not a mountain.
Dora   This ⁵**has been** / **was** a real mountain. There ⁶**has been** / **was** snow at the top. ⁷**Have you ever climbed** / **Did you ever climb** a mountain, Ivy?
Ivy   ⁸**I have** / **I did**, but not recently.

13 Interview a partner about the activities in exercise 11. Use *Have you ever …?* questions. Use the past simple to give extra information.

Have you ever climbed a mountain?

Yes I have, but not recently. It was about five years ago. Have you ever stayed in a five-star hotel?

14 Write to Dora and answer her questions. Think of some interesting things you have done. Ask Dora about her experiences.

Hi Dora

Thanks for your email. Lucky you! I haven't had a holiday recently, and I've never climbed a mountain, but last month I went to a music festival. It was amazing. Have you ever …?

Unit 11   63

Present perfect with **since** and **for**

How long have you had a cold?

Since Monday.

We use the present perfect with **since** and **for** to talk about situations and events in a period of time from the past until now.

past ←———X————————————→ now
         Monday   Tuesday   Wednesday

I**'ve had** this cold **since** Monday.
I**'ve felt** ill **for** three days.

We use **since** with a point in time (when the situation or event started).

Present perfect	since	Point in time
I've been here	since	7.30 a.m.
She's played the violin	since	she was four.

We use **for** with a length of time (the duration of the event or situation).

Present perfect	for	Length of time
I've been here	for	two hours.
She's played the violin	for	20 years.

*15 ▶11.4 **Listen and tick the correct answer.**

▶ a ☐ Since I was four.
   b ☑ Since I was ten.
1 a ☐ For five years.
   b ☐ For ten years.
2 a ☐ Since March.
   b ☐ Since April.
3 a ☐ For 30 minutes.
   b ☐ For 45 minutes.
4 a ☐ Since 2002.
   b ☐ Since 2007.
5 a ☐ Since half past two.
   b ☐ Since half past one.

*16 **Write the time expressions in the correct place.**

~~April~~ ~~ten days~~ nine o'clock 2002
two weeks a short time three years
1st October Sunday I was eight
a few minutes about half an hour

since	for
April	ten days

*17 ▶11.5 **Complete the sentences with *since* or *for*. Then listen, check and repeat.**

▶ I've known Ryan _for_ three months.
1 Have you had that book _____ you were eight?
2 We've been here _____ five minutes.
3 She's worked there _____ ten years.
4 I haven't seen you _____ August.
5 He's been ill _____ a long time.
6 She's played tennis _____ 2009.
7 They've been very happy _____ they got married.
8 You've lost weight _____ last month.

18 **Write sentences from the prompts.

▶ They / be married – 30 years
   They've been married for 30 years.
1 I / know Lucy – 2008
   _____
2 You / grow – I last saw you
   _____
3 It / not rain – two years
   _____
4 We / live here – a long time
   _____
5 He / not shave – six months
   _____
6 Her English / improve – she moved to the UK
   _____

Present perfect

19 Write questions and answers. Then interview a partner.

▶ How long / you / have / your bag?
  How long have you had your bag? *About six months.*

1 How long / you / have / that pen?

2 How long / you / be / at this school?

3 How long / you / know / your best friend?

4 How long / you / study / English?

5 How long / you / live / in your house?

20 GAME Work in pairs. Take turns to ask present perfect questions. You win a point when your friend uses an answer card. The winner is the person with the most points. You must tell the truth!

Question cards
You can use these phrases lots of times.

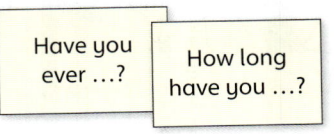

- Have you ever …?
- How long have you …?
- Have you … recently?
- How many times have you …?

Answer cards
You can only use these phrases once.

- Yes, I have.
- No, never.
- No, I haven't.
- Yes, I have.
- Since Monday.
- For 30 minutes.
- Yes, twice.
- For two weeks.
- For six months.
- Since January.
- Yes, lots of times.
- Since 2007.
- Yes, I have.
- No, I haven't.
- Since 2010.
- Since I was born.
- For a few minutes.
- Yes, I have.
- No, never.
- Since I was ten.
- Yes, I have.
- No, never.
- Yes, I have.
- Yes, I have.
- For ten minutes.

How long have you been in this room?
For 30 minutes.
That's one point for me!

Self-evaluation Rate your progress.

1–20

Unit 11

12 The future

I can recognize and use **will** and **be going to** to talk about the future.

Will and be going to

We talk about the future in different ways.

We use **be going to** when we talk about plans and predictions.
I'm going to ask the teacher for help.
It's going to be fun.

We use **be going to** + base form to talk about plans and intentions.
I'm going to wait for them.
What are we going to do?

We also use **be going to** + base form to make predictions based on evidence that we can see or feel.
Oh no! That bottle is going to fall.
I'm going to sneeze! A-tishoo!

Subject	be going to	Base form
I	'm going to	wait.
It	's going to	be fun.
We / you / they	're going to	fall.

In a few minutes I will eat this fire!

I'm not going to look.   *I'll take a photo!*

We use **will** to talk about predictions and when we make quick decisions, offers and promises.
You will love it!   *I'll phone you this evening.*

We also use the present continuous when we talk about future arrangements with other people (see unit 8).
I'm visiting my grandparents at the weekend.
He's coming home this evening.

*1 ▶ **12.1** Listen and number the pictures.

2 ▶ **12.1 Write the sentences in the correct order. Listen and check. Then listen and repeat.

▶ play / 's / going / to / the piano / he
  He's going to play the piano.

1 he / the wall / going / to / 's / paint
  _____

2 pick / they / some fruit / 're / going / to
  _____

3 he / the letter / going / 's / post / to
  _____

4 aren't / they / catch / to / the bus / going
  _____

5 to / you / 're / answer / your phone / going
  _____

66   The future

3 ▶ **12.2** Listen and answer the questions about pronunciation. Then listen again and repeat.

1 Underline the stressed (strong) words.
   a He's going to win!
   b What are you going to do?
   c They're going to help us.
   d Is it going to rain?
   e When are you going to ask her?
   f What's going to happen now?

2 How is *going to* pronounced?
   a /gəʊɪŋ tuː/ ☐
   b /gəʊɪŋ tə/ ☐

4 ▶ **12.3** Match 1–6 and a–f. Then listen and check.

▶ Why have you got all that food with you? _g_
1 Have you got any plans for the holiday? ___
2 They've knocked down the old cinema! ___
3 Are you OK? ___
4 Have you got an umbrella with you? ___
5 Have you bought a present for Sally? ___
6 Why are you wearing those old clothes? ___

a I'm going to paint the ceiling.
b No, I'm not going to give her a present.
c Yes, we're going to visit my cousins.
d No, look at the sky. It isn't going to rain.
e No, I think I'm going to be sick.
f Yes, but they're going to build a new one.
g ~~We're going to have a picnic.~~

5 What are your plans? Write a tick (✓) or a cross (✗), then write sentences with *'m (not) going to* and a time expression from the box.

| after this lesson   after school   today   this week |
| at the weekend   this afternoon   this evening |

watch TV	☐
eat some / any chocolate	☐
write some / any emails	☐
do my homework	☐
chat online	☐
play a musical instrument	☐
send some / any text messages	☐
play some / any computer games	☐

I'm going to watch TV after school.

6 Work in small groups. Compare your sentences. Who has the same plans as you?

I'm not going to eat any chocolate today.

Really? I'm going to eat some chocolate after this lesson!

Me too!

7 Work in small groups. Ask 'Why have you got that … ?' about the objects in the pictures. How many different answers with *be going to* can you think of?

apple   camera   roll of paper

rubber boots   map   umbrella

Why have you got an apple?

I'm going to eat it.

I'm going to give it to the teacher.

I'm going to cook it.

Unit 12   67

Will

We use **will** + base form to predict events and to make guesses and promises about the future.
It **will be** very expensive.
What **will** happen?
That **won't** work.   No, it **won't**.
Will it work?   Yes, it **will**.

Subject	will (not)	Base form
I / he / she / it / we / you / they	will / 'll	win.
	won't	know.

We also use **will** when we make quick decisions and offers.
I'll take the blue one, please.
I'll get you some water.

What will happen?   *I'll put them in.*

The apple will float. The key will sink to the bottom.

★8 ▶ 12.4 Listen and tick the response you hear.

▶ I'm going to try water-skiing.
☑ You'll love it.
☐ You won't like it.

1 I'm going to stay up all night.
☐ You'll feel fine tomorrow.
☐ You'll be tired tomorrow.

2 It'll be cold this evening.
☐ No, it won't.
☐ Yes, it will.

3 I'm going to do a 10 km run.
☐ It won't be difficult for you.
☐ It'll be difficult for you.

★★9 🔄▶ 12.5 Listen. Are the sounds the same (S) or different (D)?

		S	D
▶ will	still	☑	☐
▶ will	while	☐	☑
1 won't	don't	☐	☐
2 I'll	smile	☐	☐
3 won't	want	☐	☐
4 he'll	steal	☐	☐
5 she'll	shell	☐	☐
6 she'll	feel	☐	☐
7 they'll	fail	☐	☐
8 it'll	little	☐	☐

★10 ▶ 12.6 Listen and repeat.

1 She'll feel better soon.
2 It'll be a little surprise.
3 I'll smile at her.
4 Do you think he'll steal it?
5 Do you think they'll fail?
6 He won't want that.

★★11 Complete the + positive and − negative responses with *will* or *won't* and the verb in brackets. Read the conversations with a partner.

▶ 💬 I'm going to ask Jim about it.
   💬 − He _won't tell_ (tell) you.

1 💬 I'm going to see that new film at the weekend.
   💬 − You _____ (like) it.

2 💬 I'm playing tennis with Billy tomorrow.
   💬 − You _____ (win).

3 💬 It's the maths exam tomorrow. I really need to pass it.
   💬 + You _____ (pass)!

4 💬 I don't want any breakfast.
   💬 + You _____ (be) hungry later.

5 💬 I don't want to fall off my bike!
   💬 − That _____ (happen).

68   The future

✱12 Complete the conversations with the words below.

> be   cost   'll   will   will   ~~won't~~   won't   won't

▶ 💬 I think the test will be really difficult.
   💬 It _won't_.

1 💬 _____ the medicine help?
   💬 Yes, it will.
2 💬 Will it take a long time?
   💬 No, it _____. Don't worry.
3 💬 Will you _____ 13 next year?
   💬 Yes, I will. In April.
4 💬 Will it be expensive?
   💬 It will _____ about £200.
5 💬 Will he be OK?
   💬 Yes, he _____.
6 💬 Will it be dangerous?
   💬 No, it _____. You'll be fine.
7 💬 The phone's ringing!
   💬 I _____ get it!

✱13 Look and complete the predictions with *will* and *won't*.

▶ sting    2 enjoy    4 take
1 fit    3 help    5 hurt 

▶ It _will sting_ her.
1 They _____ her.
2 You _____ this.
3 That _____.
4 It _____ five minutes.
5 It _____!

✱14 Write questions about the pictures in exercise 13.

> Will it sting her?   Will they fit her?

✱15 Ask and answer the questions in small groups.

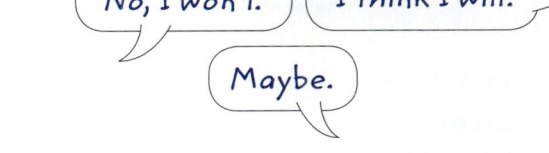

> Will it sting her? What do you think?
> No, it won't.   I think it will.
> Maybe.
>
> Will you enjoy it? What do you think?
> No, I won't.   I think I will.
> Maybe.

✱✱16 Work in pairs. Interview your partner about the future events below. Use *Will you ever …?* and the answers below.

> live in another town or city   write a book
> live in another country   record an album
> appear in a film   be rich   be famous
> play in a rock or pop band
> speak perfect English   invent something

> Do you think you'll ever live in another country?
> I think I will, but I'm not sure. Do you think you'll ever speak perfect English?
> I'm sure I will!

✓✓ I'm sure I will.
✓   I think I will, but I'm not sure.
?? I don't know. Maybe.
✗   I don't think I will.
✗✗ I'm sure I won't.

Unit 12   69

17 Look and write. What are they saying? Complete the offers of help with *'ll*, a verb and a noun.

Verbs
~~clean~~ cut fix make
pick up plant wash

Nouns
the books some new curtains the floor
the grass the shelf some flowers ~~the windows~~

▶ Jack I'<u>'ll clean the windows</u>.
1 Oscar I _____.
2 Ed and Sue We _____.
3 Linda I _____.
4 Gemma I _____.
5 Mike and Molly We _____.
6 Charlie I _____.

18 **GAME** How much can you remember? Who's going to do what? Cover the picture in exercise 17 and write the action plan.

ACTION PLAN

▶ Jack <u>is going to clean the windows</u>.
1 Oscar _____.
2 Ed and Sue _____.
3 Linda _____.
4 Gemma _____.
5 Mike and Molly _____.
6 Charlie _____.

19 Circle the correct form, *will* or *be going to*.

▶ 💬 What are your plans for the weekend?
  💬 I**('m going to)**/ 'll tidy my bedroom.
1 💬 Which of these notebooks would you like?
  💬 Erm… I**'m going to** / **'ll** have that one, please.
2 💬 Have you thought about it?
  💬 Yes, I have. So, what **are you going to** / **will you** do?
3 💬 They**'ll** / **'re going to** get married.
  💬 Really? When did they decide that?
4 💬 I can't do this.
  💬 I**'m going to** / **'ll** help you.
5 💬 It's a secret.
  💬 I know. I promise I**'m not going to** / **won't** tell anyone.

70 The future

20 Work with a partner. Look at the choices. Decide who will do what.

1 wash up / dry up
2 have the fruit salad / have the cake
3 make the cake / decorate the cake
4 chop the salad / make a sandwich
5 write the story / draw the pictures
6 hold the ladder / climb the ladder

I'll wash up.
But I hate drying up!
OK. I'll dry up.

21 Complete the email with *will* or *be going to* and a verb from the box.

attend be be do do have
not be pack phone send ~~write~~

Hi there

This will be a short email, I'm afraid. (I promise I'll write _____ again soon!)

I hope you're enjoying the holiday so far.

I'm writing to say that I ¹_____ at home for the next six weeks because I've made an important decision. I ²_____ summer camp this year.

I ³_____ very busy tonight and tomorrow. I ⁴_____ a 'goodbye' meal with my family this evening, and tomorrow I ⁵_____ my bags. I also need to do some shopping before I go – toothpaste, a notebook, things like that. Help! I've got so much to do!

I ⁶_____ you a postcard and I ⁷_____ you in a few weeks, OK? Is your number still 07444 117816?

What ⁸_____ (you) this summer? Email me with your plans!

George

P.S. This is my summer homework task: 'Where do you think you ⁹_____ 10 years from now? What do you think you ¹⁰_____ every day?' So, how about you, 10 years from now? Tell me.

22 Write back to George. Include the information below.

Your plans for tonight and tomorrow
Your plans for the summer
Your predictions about your life 10 years from now
Offer to help George with his preparations

Dear George

I'm sure you'll have a wonderful time at summer camp. I …

Self-evaluation Rate your progress.

	😊	😊😊	😊😊😊
1			
2			
3			
4			
5			
6			
7			
8			
9			
10			
11			
12			
13			
14			
15			
16			
17			
18			
19			
20			
21			
22			

13 Imperatives

I can recognize and use imperatives.

We use imperatives to give warnings, instructions and directions.

Imperatives are the same as the base form.
Eat this.   **Be** careful!   Always **cross** the road carefully.

We begin negative imperatives with **Don't**, **Do not**, or **Never**:
Don't say that!   **Do not open** this window.
Never touch that plant.

We use **please** with imperatives to make them more polite.
Please come here.   **Don't do** that, **please**.

LOOK OUT!

Be quiet! Don't shout in the library!

*1 ▶13.1 Listen and number.

*2 ▶13.2 Match 1–9 with a–j. Listen and check. Then listen and repeat.

▶ Look	d	a me.
1 Be	___	b worry.
2 Wash	___	c a circle.
3 Wait	___	d̶ o̶u̶t̶!
4 Turn	___	e well!
5 Follow	___	f holiday!
6 Don't	___	g careful!
7 Draw	___	h for me!
8 Sleep	___	i right.
9 Have a good	___	j your hands.

*3 Write these classroom instructions in the correct order.

▶ to / listen / me
   Listen to me.

1 the / read / story
   _____

2 name / write / your
   _____

3 and / repeat / listen
   _____

4 use / don't / a pencil
   _____

5 with / your partner / talk
   _____

6 a dictionary / don't / use
   _____

7 at page 9 / your books / open
   _____

8 your homework / don't / forget
   _____

9 quiet / be
   _____

72   Imperatives

*4 Look and match the directions to the pictures. You don't have to use all the directions.

Take the second right.   Don't turn left.   Turn right.   Open the gate.   ~~Go north.~~
Go straight ahead.   Walk south.   Walk east.   Go west.   Cross the bridge.

▶ Go north.
1 _____
2 _____
3 _____
4 _____
5 _____

5 GAME Find your way through the maze! Work with a partner.

1 Put your counter on START.
2 Follow the instructions.
3 Move one square at a time.
4 Which colour square do you finish on?

START
GO EAST

GO SOUTH
GO WEST
TURN LEFT
DON'T GO EAST OR WEST
GO EAST
GO SOUTH
DON'T GO ANYWHERE

TURN AROUND
DON'T GO ONTO A YELLOW SQUARE
TURN RIGHT
TURN AROUND
GO STRAIGHT ON
GO BACKWARDS
DON'T GO ONTO A YELLOW OR GREEN SQUARE
DON'T GO ANYWHERE

GO AHEAD FOUR SQUARES
TURN LEFT
DON'T GO EAST, NORTH OR SOUTH
TURN LEFT
MOVE ONTO THE NEXT PINK SQUARE
GO AHEAD THREE SQUARES
DON'T MOVE
DON'T GO ANYWHERE

TURN RIGHT
GO EAST
GO AHEAD TWO SQUARES
DON'T GO WEST OR SOUTH
DON'T GO ONTO A GREEN SQUARE
DON'T GO ONTO A GREEN OR BLUE SQUARE
TURN LEFT
DON'T GO ANYWHERE

Unit 13 73

6 ▶ 13.3 Treasure hunt! You are at the station. Listen to the directions and mark ✗ on the map for the treasure.

7 ▶ 13.3 Listen again and tick ✓ the correct instruction.

- ▶ a ✓ Leave the station.
- b ☐ Don't leave the station.
- 1 a ☐ Walk north.
- b ☐ Walk south.
- 2 a ☐ Walk to the river.
- b ☐ Don't walk to the river.
- 3 a ☐ Cross the bridge.
- b ☐ Don't cross the bridge.
- 4 a ☐ Turn left.
- b ☐ Turn right.
- 5 a ☐ Open the gate.
- b ☐ Don't open the gate.
- 6 a ☐ Dig in the ground.
- b ☐ Look on the ground.

8 Mystery Tour! Give directions and follow directions. Student A go to page 154. Student B follow student A's directions.

Go out of the station. Walk south to the river. Cross the bridge and …

9 GAME Choose a place on the map to hide your treasure. Keep it a secret. Write directions. Give your directions to another student. Can he or she find the treasure?

Leave the station.

Walk to the beach.

Take the second right and …

74 Imperatives

10 Complete the rules in the notices. Use the positive or negative imperative of the verbs in the boxes.

return   ~~speak~~   use   write

Dos and don'ts at the library

Please …
1 ✓ _Speak_ quietly.
2 ✓ _____ your books on time.
3 ✗ _____ the photocopier.
4 ✗ _____ in the library books.

eat   enjoy   switch off   take   touch

Dos and don'ts at the art gallery

Please …
5 ✓ _____ this collection of paintings.
6 ✓ _____ your mobile phone.
7 ✗ _____ the paintings.
8 ✗ _____ any food.
9 ✗ _____ photos of the paintings.

keep   light   pick   play   put

Dos and don'ts at the park

Please …
10 ✓ _____ your dog on a lead.
11 ✓ _____ your litter in the bin.
12 ✗ _____ loud music.
13 ✗ _____ fires.
14 ✗ _____ the flowers.

11 Work in groups. Make a poster of your school's rules. Use the ideas below and your own ideas.

The classroom
mobile phone   listen   polite   on time / late

The playground
litter   walk / run

The canteen
shout   wait   take   eat

Dos and don'ts at our school

In the classroom
Please …
✓ _switch off your mobile phone._
✓ _____
✓ _____
✓ _____

Please …
✗ _don't arrive late._
✗ _____
✗ _____
✗ _____

In the playground
Please …
_____
_____

In the canteen
_____

Self-evaluation Rate your progress.

1
2
3
4
5
6
7
8
9
10
11

Unit 13   75

Mini-revision Units 11–13

Reading and writing

1 What does Henry say to Tim? Match a letter (a–h) with 1–5. You don't need to use all the letters.

Henry f
▶ Tim No, never.
1 Henry ____
  Tim Do you think so?
2 Henry ____
  Tim That's good. But what about jellyfish? And are there any sharks?
3 Henry ____
  Tim Good. I think I'm ready … I'm just a bit nervous.
4 Henry ____
  Tim OK.
5 Henry ____
  Tim Yes, it's beautiful. Let's go!

a You won't remember.
b I've never seen any here.
c I haven't been here recently.
d Don't worry! You'll be fine.
e Yes. We're going to see all kinds of fish.
f ~~Have you ever been scuba diving before?~~
g Never? You'll love it.
h Look at the colour of the water!

2 Read the email and write the missing words. Write one word on each line.

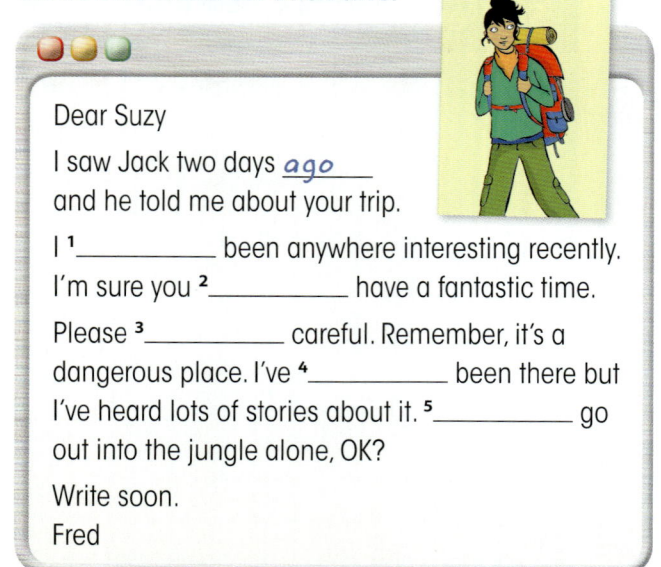

Dear Suzy
I saw Jack two days *ago*
and he told me about your trip.
I ¹_____ been anywhere interesting recently.
I'm sure you ²_____ have a fantastic time.
Please ³_____ careful. Remember, it's a dangerous place. I've ⁴_____ been there but I've heard lots of stories about it. ⁵_____ go out into the jungle alone, OK?
Write soon.
Fred

Listening

3 ▶ R6.1 Listen and tick ✓ the correct picture.
▶ Which is Mary's house?

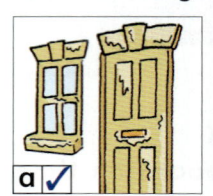

1 Which is Mary's street?

2 Which picture is William Carter?

3 Which picture is Mrs Basset?

Speaking

4 Talk with a partner. Look. Who says these things to you?

1 You'll be cold!
2 You've done very well at school recently.
3 Stop talking!
4 Have you done your homework?
5 Hurry up!
6 Have you tidied your bedroom?
7 Be careful!
8 You're going to be late!

My brother always says 'Hurry up!' My mum always says …

Revision 3 — Units 8–13

Reading and writing

1 Look and read. Write 'yes' or 'no'.

▶ It's raining. _no_
1 The football's broken the window. _____
2 The boy with black hair's going to write on the board. _____
3 It will be Tuesday 12th June tomorrow. _____
4 The red and white sign on the door means 'Don't talk.' _____
5 Two people are wearing glasses. _____
6 The class is visiting the science museum on Friday 22nd June. _____
7 The girl with long hair has just dropped her book. _____

2 Read the letter and circle the correct answers.

Dear Charlie

I (**'m writing**) / write / wrote to you from my hotel room. I ¹ was arriving / have arrived / arrived here yesterday afternoon. Unfortunately, I didn't ² have / had / having a very good journey. Lots of other people ³ were travelling / travelled / have travelled yesterday, so the roads and airports were very busy.

My room is nice but I couldn't ⁴ sleeping / sleep / slept last night. People ⁵ are making / were making / made a lot of noise outside my window. It was terrible.

Tomorrow we ⁶ 're exploring / explore / explored the Ancient City. I think it ⁷ was / has been / will be very interesting.

I'll write again soon. ⁸ Saying / Said / Say 'hello' to Nina from me.

Betty

P.S. The restaurant ⁹ 's getting / gets / got noisy again. I think I ¹⁰ ask / 'm asking / 'll ask the manager for a different room.

Revision 3   77

Listening

3 ▶ **R7.1** Listen and draw lines.

David   Jane   Jim   Suzy   Andy   Billy   Oscar

Speaking

4 Work in pairs. Ask and answer questions about Jack Smith, then ask and answer questions about you and your partner.

Name	Jack Smith
Where / live	in the city centre
What / studying	Spanish and maths
ever / had a job	no, never
What / doing / this time last year	studying in Argentina
When will / finish / studies	next summer

Name	
Where / live	
What / studying	
ever / had a job	
What / doing / this time last year	
When will / finish / studies	

14 Can and could for ability and permission

I can recognize and use **can** and **could** for ability and permission.

Can and could for ability

I can skateboard really well!

But I can't skateboard here.

NO SKATEBOARDING

Can and **could** are modal verbs. We use them to talk about possibility, ability and permission. We use **can** and **can't** to talk about our present abilities.

Subject	can / can't	Base form
I / he / she / it / we / you / they	can can't	swim 1000 metres. dance.

Can	Subject	Base form
Can	I / we / she / it / we / you / they	swim 1000 metres? dance?

We use **could** and **couldn't** to talk about our abilities in the past. We often use a past time phrase.

Subject	could / couldn't	Base form	Past time phrase
I / he / she / it / we / you / they	could couldn't	swim	when I was eight. when she was three. this morning. yesterday. in 2006.

We often use **can** and **could** for ability to talk about our senses.
I **can smell** smoke.   I **can't taste** it.
Can you **hear** me?   I **couldn't see** it.

*1 ▶ 14.1 Listen and tick ✓ the correct picture.

▶ What can Sarah do?
a ✓   b ☐   c ☐

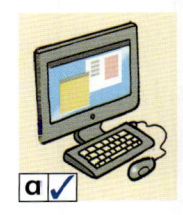

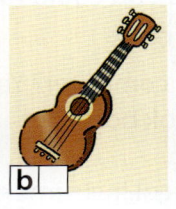

1 Why is Max late?
a ☐   b ☐   c ☐

2 What was the weather like this morning?
a ☐   b ☐   c ☐

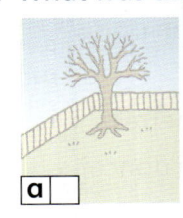

3 Where's Sarah?
a ☐   b ☐   c ☐

4 How far can Emily's dad run?
a ☐   b ☐   c ☐

5 What can Edward cook?
a ☐   b ☐   c ☐

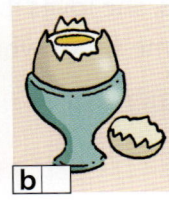

Unit 14   79

2 ▶ 14.2 Match 1–8 with a–i, then listen and check. Practise saying the sentences.

▶ Can you play — d
1 I couldn't find — ___
2 I could say — ___
3 I couldn't see — ___
4 I can hear — ___
5 Can you design things — ___
6 I can't hear — ___
7 Emily's dad could run — ___
8 I can't cook — ___

a on the computer? Yes, I can.
b my book bag.
c an egg.
d ~~a musical instrument? No, I can't.~~
e the tree at the end of the garden.
f some birds and the sea.
g some words in Spanish when I was four.
h any cars or people.
i 10 km fifteen years ago.

3 Complete the conversations with *can*, *can't*, *could* or *couldn't*. Then act the conversations in pairs.

▶ 💬 How far _can_ you run?
   💬 About two kilometres.
1 💬 _____ you dance?
   💬 No, but I _____ when I was young.
2 💬 How did you know there was a fire?
   💬 I _____ see lots of smoke.
3 💬 Does Leo know how to cook?
   💬 No, he _____ even make a sandwich!
4 💬 Did you ride your bike yesterday?
   💬 No, I didn't. It was broken and I _____ fix it.
5 💬 What's that noise?
   💬 What noise? I _____ hear anything.
6 💬 Does Libby like playing the piano?
   💬 Yes, she loves it. She _____ play some songs when she was three.

4 Write eight sentences using words and phrases from below. Write some sentences about now and some about the past. Write some sentences that are true and some that aren't true.

I can skateboard.
I could swim when I was four.

I
can
can't
could
couldn't

swim underwater
speak English
use a computer
skateboard
cook an egg
ride a bike
make a cake
play a musical instrument
do a headstand

when I was four / five / six …
in 2006

5 GAME Work in groups. Read your sentences to the other students. Can they guess which sentences are true for you?

I can cook an egg. *That's not true.*
It is true! I can cook an egg!

80 **Can** and **could** for ability and permission

Can and could for permission

You can watch another film ...

... but you can't have any more chocolate.

Can we shut the door, Dad?

Could I go to the bathroom, please?

We use **can** and **can't** to give and refuse permission.

| You | can | go ... |
| | can't | have ... |

We use **can** and **could** to ask for permission. **Could** is more formal than **can**.

| Can | I | have ...? |
| Could | we | go ...? |

*6 Complete the sentences with *can* or *can't*.

▶ You _can't_ use your phone here.

1 You _____ listen to music here.

2 You _____ take photos here.

3 You _____ play ball games here.

*7 Write one rule with *can* and one rule with *can't* for each place.

at the cinema   at the library   at school
on a plane   at the zoo   at the museum

You can't talk at the cinema.

**8 GAME Work in groups. Choose one of the places in exercise 7. Say the rules but don't say the place! Can the other students guess the place?

You can eat sweets. You can't talk.

At the cinema?

Yes, that's right.

Unit 14

9 Tick ✓ the correct answer.

▶ Can I ___ it now?
  a ☐ to eat   b ✓ eat

1 No, you ___ use your mobile phone in class.
  a ☐ can   b ☐ can't

2 ___ say something, please?
  a ☐ I could   b ☐ Could I

3 Yes, you ___ go to the party.
  a ☐ can   b ☐ could

4 I'm sorry. You ___ play football here.
  a ☐ can't   b ☐ couldn't

5 Excuse me, Mrs Bond, ___ I photocopy this?
  a ☐ could   b ☐ can't

6 Could I take this book home, please?
  a ☐ I'm sorry but you couldn't.
  b ☐ I'm sorry but you can't.

10 ▶ 14.3 Listen to the conversations. Is each answer *yes* ✓ or *no* ✗?

▶ ✓
1 ☐
2 ☐
3 ☐
4 ☐
5 ☐

11 ▶ 14.4 Listen again for these responses. Then put them in the correct place.

~~Go ahead.~~   No, you can't.   Of course.
OK.   I'm afraid not.   Sorry, no.
Of course you can.

Yes	No
Go ahead.	

12 Work in pairs. Ask your partner's permission to do something. Use ideas from exercises 8 and 10, and your own ideas. Your partner will give or refuse permission.

Can I take photos here?

No, I'm afraid not.

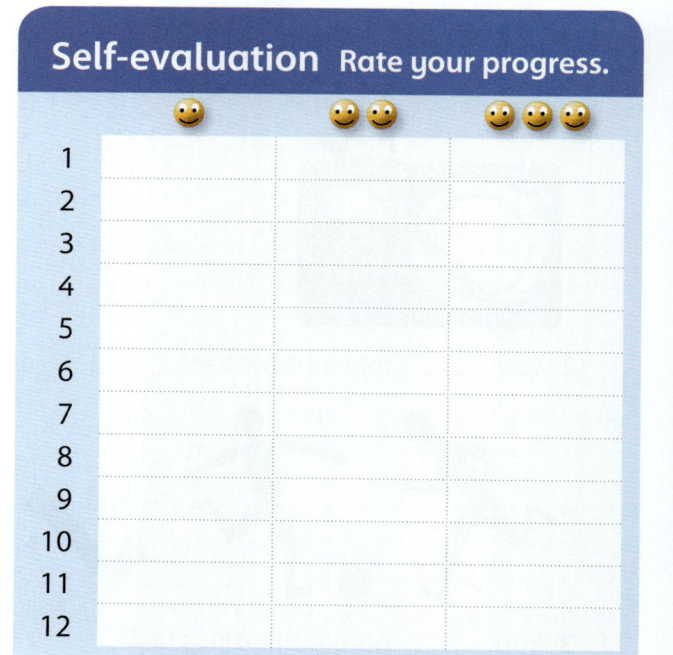

Self-evaluation Rate your progress.

1
2
3
4
5
6
7
8
9
10
11
12

82 **Can** and **could** for ability and permission

15 Might and may

I can recognize and use **may** and **might** for possibility, and **may** for permission.

Might and may for possibility

That balloon might land here. May I use the binoculars now?

Might and **may** are modal verbs. We use **might** and **may** to talk about something that is possible, but not definite.

Subject	might (not) / may (not)	Base form
It	might	land here.
She	may	want help.

We use **might / may** and **might not / may not** to talk about present possibilities.

is — might (may) be — might (may) not be — isn't

There **might** be a message on it.
James **may** have a pen.

We also use **might / may** and **might not / may not** to talk about future possibilities.

will — might (may) — might (may) not — won't

You **might** hurt someone.
It **may** land here.

We often use **I think ...** with **might / may** and **might not / may not** when we are not sure about the possibilities.
I think I **might** go home now.

*1 ▶ 15.1 What might happen? Complete the sentences with the endings below. Then listen and check.

~~eat it~~   pop   help you   be a fox   see a rainbow

▶ The cat might _eat it_ !

1 I think this might _____.

2 We might _____.

3 Is it a dog? It might _____.

4 The balloon might _____!

**2 Are the sentences in exercise 1 about a present (P) or future (F) possibility? Write P or F.

▶ _P_   1 ___   2 ___   3 ___   4 ___

Unit 15   83

3 ▶ 15.2 Listen and repeat.

might /maɪt/: weak 't'
It might be a fox.
I might not finish it.

might /maɪt/: strong 't'
The cat might eat it.
I might ask the teacher.

4 Match rules 1–2 with a–b.

1 We pronounce a strong final 't' in **might** ___
2 We don't pronounce a strong final 't' in **might** ___

a when the main verb begins with a vowel sound.
b when the main verb begins with a consonant sound.

5 ▶ 15.3 Read the sentences. Is the final 't' in *might* strong? Tick ✓ or cross ✗, then listen and check.

▶ I might keep this card. ✗
1 He might buy it. ☐
2 I might ask the teacher. ☐
3 She might agree with you. ☐
4 Do you think we might win? ☐
5 I might act in the school play this year. ☐
6 I might eat it later. ☐
7 They might not want it. ☐

6 ▶ 15.4 Add responses a–e to the conversations in pictures 1–4. Listen and check, then act out the conversations with a partner.

a It might be in your bag.
b I think you might have flu.
c Do you think it might be Carla?
d ~~It might snow.~~
e It might be a present for me!

▶ Look at those clouds. — d

1 The postman's bringing a big parcel. — ___

2 I feel terrible. — ___

3 There's someone at the door. — ___

4 I can't find my phone. — ___

84 **Might** and **may**

May for permission

We can use **may** in questions to ask for permission. We also use **could** but **may** is more formal.

May I have a go?

Of course. Go ahead.

*7 ▶ 15.5 Listen and number the conversations 1–6.

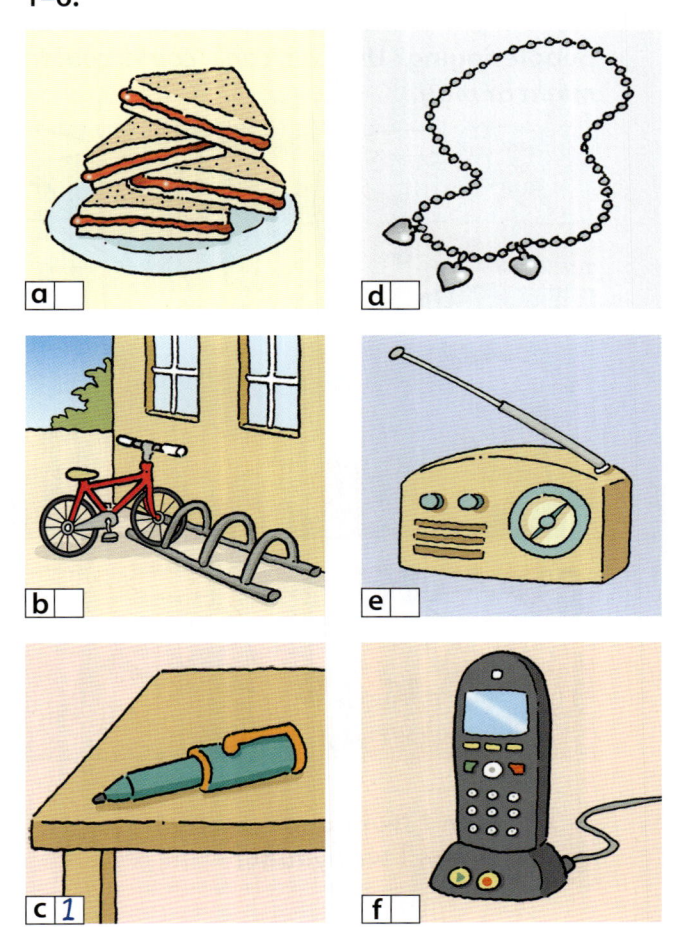

a ☐
d ☐
b ☐
e ☐
c 1
f ☐

*8 Write the questions in the correct order. Then practise the conversations with a partner.

▶ I / ask / a question / may

May I ask a question?

Yes, go ahead. What is it?

1 borrow / I / your / may / dictionary

_____?

Yes, of course.

2 photocopier / may / use / I / the

_____?

I'm afraid it's not working at the moment.

3 my bike / here / leave / I / may

_____?

Yes, of course. It'll be fine here.

4 have / may / a cake / I

_____?

No, you may not! You've just had breakfast!

Self-evaluation Rate your progress.

	🙂	🙂🙂	🙂🙂🙂
1			
2			
3			
4			
5			
6			
7			
8			

Unit 15   85

Mini-revision Units 14–15

Reading and writing

1 Look and read. Choose the correct words and write them on the lines.

bee   bird   chameleon
horse   panda   scorpion

▶ It can fly and it can sing. _bird_
1 You might see this large animal on a farm. It can run very fast. _____
2 You can see this black and white animal at the zoo. _____
3 You might not see this animal because it can change its colour. _____
4 It can fly. It makes honey. _____
5 You might see this small animal in the desert. It can't fly. It might sting you. _____

2 Read the email. Choose the correct words from the box to complete the text.

~~can~~   can't   could   couldn't   go   might

Dear Kim

Please come and visit me! You _can_ come any time – I'm not doing anything! I'm feeling much better now but I still ¹_____ walk very much. It's so frustrating! The doctors said they ²_____ take the plaster off in three weeks but they aren't sure. That means I might not ³_____ back to school before the summer holidays. ⁴_____ you do something for me? I need my notebooks from school. I asked Jack but he ⁵_____ find them. I think they're on a shelf in the classroom. Thank you!

Emily

Listening

3 ▶ R8.1 Listen and draw lines.

Richard   Lucy   Angie   Martin

Billy   Dora   Sam

Speaking

4 Work in pairs. Look at the pictures. What are the people saying? Use *can*, *can't*, *could*, *couldn't*, *might* **or** *may*.

I couldn't swim underwater when I was young!

86 Units 14–15

16 Have to, must, and shall

I can recognize and use **have to** and **must** for obligation, **mustn't** for prohibition and **shall** for offers.

Have to and don't have to

Have to and **don't have to** are modal verbs. We use **have to** to talk about things that are important because of rules and situations.
My sister **has to** wear a school uniform.
I **have to** wear glasses. My eyes aren't good.

We use **don't have to** to talk about things that are not necessary.
You **don't have to** buy a ticket.
He **doesn't have to** work.

Shall I tidy the garden for you?
That's very kind of you, but you don't have to.
I'd like to.
OK, but you mustn't work too hard!

Subject	(don't) have to	Base form
I / we / you / they	have to / don't have to	leave now. work. go.
He / she / it	has to / doesn't have to	

Do / Does	Subject	have to	Base form
Do	I / we / you / they	have to	stop?
Does	he / she / it		

Do you **have to** work?   Yes, I do. / No, I don't.
Does she **have to** study?   Yes, she does. / No, she doesn't.

*1 ▶ 16.1 Listen to the conversation. Then listen and repeat.
Heidi: It's half past three! I have to go.
Andy: Do you have to go right now?
Heidi: Yes, I do. I have to be home at four.

*2 ↻▶ 16.2 Listen again and answer the question. Then act out the conversation with a partner.
How do we pronounce **have to**?
a /hæv tə/ ☐   b /hæf tə/ ☐

**3 ▶ 16.3 Listen and tick ✓ the correct picture.

Unit 16   87

4 Complete the questions with the correct verbs.

cook take pay phone ~~wear~~ wear

▶ Does she have to _wear_ a tie?
1 Do you have to _____ the beans?
2 Does she have to _____ Jim at nine?
3 Does he have to _____ the medicine four times a day?
4 Do you have to _____ special boots?
5 Do you have to _____ to go into the park?

5 Complete the text with *has to*, *have to*, *doesn't have to* or *don't have to*.

My family
My dad works in a factory. He _has to_ get up very early. My mum works in a shop. She ¹_____ take the bus to work. She and the other shop workers ²_____ wear a green uniform. My brother and I ³_____ take the bus to school. We ⁴_____ pay. We have a special bus pass from school. My little sister is only two so she ⁵_____ go to school yet.

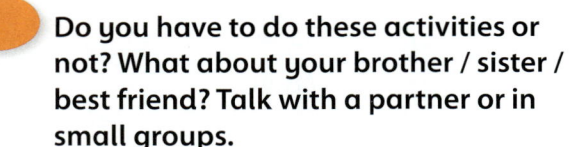

6 Do you have to do these activities or not? What about your brother / sister / best friend? Talk with a partner or in small groups.

do homework every day
keep the house clean
keep my bedroom neat and tidy
take a bus or train to school
help with the cooking
help in the garden

My brother has to do homework every day.

I don't have to take a bus or train to school.

7 🎵 16.4 Read and add the missing verbs. Listen and check. Then listen and repeat.

cook do keep pay ~~spend~~
teach work work write

I don't have to _spend_ all day on my feet.
I don't have to ¹_____ and
²_____ the house neat.
I don't have to ³_____ for the food that I eat.
I've got an easy life!

You're not a parent, that is true.
You don't have to do what parents do.
You don't have to work.
You study and play …
… but you might become a parent one day!

I might become a parent, that's very true.
And then I'll do the things that parents do.
I might become a parent, you're quite right.
And then I'll have to ⁴_____ hard – day and night!

I don't have to ⁵_____ on the board with a pen.
I don't have to ⁶_____ things again and again.
I don't have to ⁷_____ every evening till ten.
I've got an easy life!

You're not a teacher, that is true.
You don't have to do what teachers do.
You don't have to work.
You study and play …
… but you might become a teacher one day!

I might become a teacher, that's very true.
And then I'll do the things that teachers do.
I might become a teacher, you're quite right.
And then I'll have to ⁸_____ hard – day and night!

Have to, must, and shall

Must and mustn't

Must and mustn't are modal verbs. We use must and mustn't in rules and to give orders.

Subject	must / mustn't	Base form
You	must	wait here.
You	mustn't	be late.

We use **must** to talk about obligation. **Must** is similar to **have to**.
You **must** be there at nine o'clock.
You **must** write in black ink.

Mustn't is similar to **can't**.
You **mustn't** run in the school.
You **mustn't** bring your phone to school.

To ask about obligation we usually use **Do I have to ... ?**, not **Must I ... ?**
Do I have to be there at nine o'clock?
Do I have to write in black ink?

*8 16.5 Listen. Do we pronounce the 't' in *must*? Then listen and repeat.

▶ You must arrive on time. (yes) / no
1 You must eat everything. yes / no
2 You must open the door. yes / no
3 You must learn these facts. yes / no
4 You must bring a hat. yes / no
5 You mustn't say that. yes / no
6 You mustn't argue. yes / no

**9 16.6 Who is saying 1–8? Guess and match. Listen and check.

a sports teacher   f ~~police officer~~
b parent   g doctor
c music teacher   h bus driver
d museum attendant   i science teacher
e dentist

▶ You must have lights on your bike at night. _f_
1 You must tidy your bedroom. ___
2 You must eat a lot of fruit and vegetables. ___
3 You must try to run faster. ___
4 You must listen to the beat. ___
5 You must sit down when we're moving. ___
6 You mustn't take photos in here. ___
7 You mustn't touch these chemicals. ___
8 You mustn't eat so much chocolate. ___

*10 Look at the pictures. Circle the correct answer.

▶ You (must) / mustn't stop here.
1 You must / mustn't pay £5 to go in.
2 You must / mustn't run.
3 You must / mustn't swim here.
4 You must / mustn't be over 13 to go in.
5 You must / mustn't turn right.

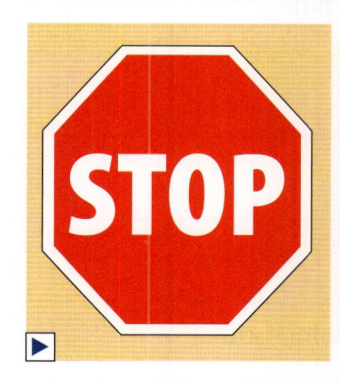

Unit 16   89

11 Look at the signs and write sentences with *must* and *mustn't*.

▶ cross the road
You mustn't cross the road.

1 turn left
___

2 show your ticket
___

3 put rubbish in the bin
___

4 walk on the paths
___

5 light fires
___

6 take birds' eggs
___

7 close the gates behind you
___

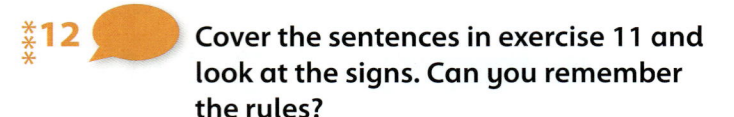

12 Cover the sentences in exercise 11 and look at the signs. Can you remember the rules?

> You mustn't cross the road.

13 GAME Work in groups. How many rules can you write for these places? Use *must* and *mustn't*. Which group can think of the most rules?

the city   the countryside   a museum
the science classroom   the sports field
your classroom

> In the city you must stop at red lights.

> You must use pedestrian crossings.

> You mustn't drop rubbish on the pavement.

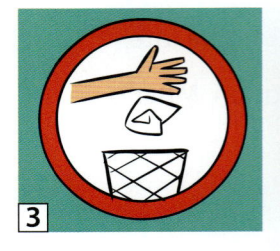

14 What do people say to you? Write sentences with *must* and *mustn't*.

> You must wear a hat.
> You mustn't eat lots of sweets.

15 Work with a partner. Can your partner guess who says the sentences in exercise 14?

> You must wear a hat. I think your mum says that.

> No, my dad says that.

16 Circle the correct answers.

▶ **Must you** / **(Do you have to)** wear black shoes to school?

1 You **mustn't** / **don't have to** use the photocopier. It's only for teachers.

2 You sit on the sofa all the time. You **must** / **don't have to** take some exercise!

3 You **mustn't** / **don't have to** take a bus. You can walk there.

4 I **must** / **have to** get up at six o'clock every day.

90   Have to, must, and shall

Shall for offers

We use **Shall I ...** + base form to make offers.
Shall I carry your bag?
Shall I make lunch?

Look at these replies:

to say 'yes'
Yes, please.
Thank you very much.
That would be nice. Thank you.

to say 'no'
It's OK, thanks.
No, don't worry.
I'm OK, thanks.
I can manage.

Speech bubbles:
- I don't feel well.
- Shall I sing you a song?
- No, don't worry.
- Shall I tell you a story?
- No, it's OK thanks.
- Shall I stop talking?
- Yes, that would be very nice.

*17 Write the words in the correct order to make offers.

▶ a photo / shall / take / I
  <u>Shall I take a photo?</u>

1 the door / shall / I / close
  _____

2 wait for / I / shall / you
  _____

3 tell you / I / the answer / shall
  _____

4 shall / a clue / I / give you
  _____

***18 Work in pairs and have conversations. Use these ideas or your own.

switch the TV on   sing you a song   light a fire
tell you a joke   get you a drink   tell my mum

▶ I'm bored.
1 I'm worried about my sister.
2 I've got a really bad headache.
3 I can't use this camera.
4 I'm thirsty.
5 I'm cold.

- I'm bored.   Shall I switch the TV on?
- No, don't worry.   Shall I ...

Self-evaluation Rate your progress.

	😊	😊😊	😊😊😊
1			
2			
3			
4			
5			
6			
7			
8			
9			
10			
11			
12			
13			
14			
15			
16			
17			
18			

17 Should

I can recognize and use **should** and **shouldn't** for giving opinions and advice.

We use **should** to give opinions and advice.

Subject	should (not)	Base form
I / he / she / it / we / you / they	should shouldn't	tell him. be here.

We **should** get a taxi.
You **shouldn't** do that.

We form questions like this.

should	Subject	Base form
Should	I / he / she / it / we / you / they	leave? open it?

Should I tell Dave? Yes, you **should**.
What **should** I do?

We often use **I think …** and **I don't think …** with **should**.
I think he **should** leave now.
I don't think you **should** eat a lot of sweets.

The door should be in the middle, there should be more windows and the garden should be bigger.

You should become an architect!

---

*1 ▶ **17.1** Look and read. Circle the correct answers. Then listen and check.

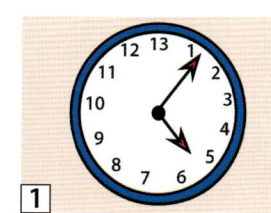

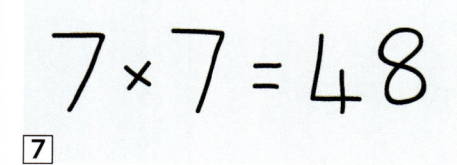

▶ The fish **should** / (**shouldn't**) have legs.

1. The clock **should** / **shouldn't** have twelve numbers.
2. They shouldn't have **short** / **long** ears.
3. It **should** / **shouldn't** have six numbers.
4. It should have **two** / **four** legs.
5. They shouldn't be **pink** / **grey**.
6. The diary **should** / **shouldn't** say 'Monday, Tuesday, Wednesday'.
7. The answer should be **49** / **48**.

$7 \times 7 = 48$

*2 **GAME** Work in pairs. Cover the sentences in exercise 1. How many sentences can you remember?

3 Work in pairs. Look. How many things are in the wrong place? Where should they be?

in / on the …
cage sofa vase fish tank fridge microwave
CD rack mantlepiece wall shelf floor table

The cushion should be on the sofa.

And the fish …

4 ▶ 17.2 Listen and number the conversations 1–4.

a
b 1
c
d

5 ▶ 17.2 Listen again and complete the conversations with *should* or *shouldn't*. Act out the conversations with a partner.

▶ ○ <u>Should</u> I buy it?
   ○ I don't know. Maybe.
1 ○ _____ I take the flowers?
   ○ Yes, why not?
2 ○ _____ he stop? What do you think?
   ○ No, he _____ keep going.
     He _____ stop now.
3 ○ What _____ he do?
   ○ He _____ move his head. The girl _____ phone for help.

6 Complete the sentences with *should* and verbs from the box below.

be be eat ~~have~~ have
help learn play work

▶ Teenagers <u>should have</u> computers in their bedrooms.
1 People _____ meat.
2 There _____ more public holidays.
3 Teenagers _____ credit cards.
4 Boys and girls _____ with the housework.
5 Teenagers _____ one day a week.
6 All boys _____ cooking.
7 All girls _____ football.
8 Every weekend _____ three days, not two.

7 Do you agree or disagree with the opinions in exercise 6? Work in pairs or small groups. Compare your answers. Use *I think …* and *I don't think …*

I don't think teenagers should have their computers in their bedrooms.

Really? Why not? Teenagers use computers to do their homework.

Unit 17   93

8 Complete the sentences with *should* or *shouldn't* and the words in brackets.

▶ It's cold outside. You <u>should wear</u> (wear) a hat.
1 I _____ (eat) any more chocolate. I'll feel sick.
2 _____ (I / stand) up or sit down?
3 You _____ (sit) so close to the TV. It's bad for your eyes.
4 You _____ (touch) that. The paint's not completely dry yet.
5 That was very kind of him. You _____ (write) a thank-you letter.
6 You _____ (do) what you promised to do.
7 I don't think they _____ (be) in the swimming pool.
8 _____ (she / tell) the teacher?
9 He _____ (do) that. It's very dangerous.
10 _____ (we / leave) now?

9 Look at the pictures. Talk about what the people should and shouldn't do.

I think he should buy another ice cream.

Yes, and he should be careful next time!

10 Read the text messages and write replies. Give advice.

Hi, I'm really worried about the exam tomorrow. I think I'm going to stay up all night and study. Jenny

Hi, Can you believe this? I found a purse in the street today – and it's got LOTS of money in it! Vicky says I should take it to the police. What do you think? Ed

Hi, I need your advice. Tim was copying answers from Charlie's paper in the exam today. Should I tell Mr Paul? Polly

Hi, Emma invited me to her party on Saturday and I said 'yes'. But now Claire has invited me to her party on the same night. I really want to go to Claire's party. What should I do?

Hi Jenny
I think you should ...

Self-evaluation Rate your progress.

	😊	😊😊	😊😊😊😊
1			
2			
3			
4			
5			
6			
7			
8			
9			
10			

94 Should

Mini-revision   Units 16–17

Reading and writing

1 Read the email. Choose the right words and write them on the lines.

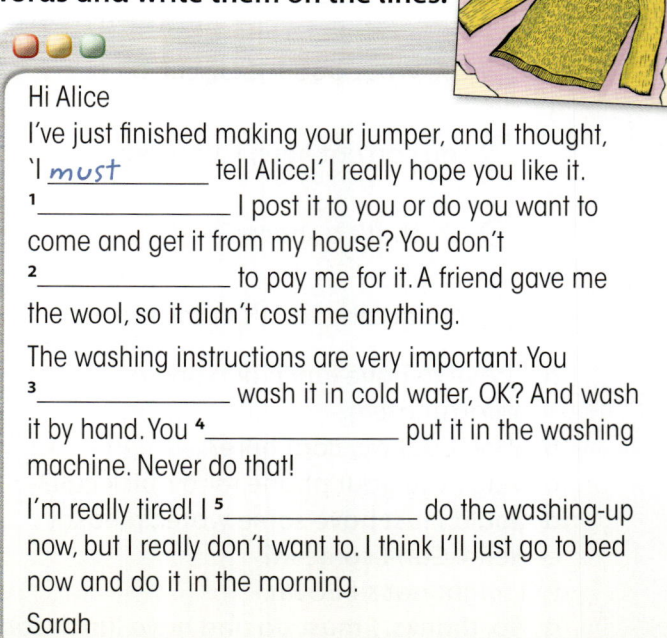

Hi Alice
I've just finished making your jumper, and I thought, 'I _must_ tell Alice!' I really hope you like it. ¹_____ I post it to you or do you want to come and get it from my house? You don't ²_____ to pay me for it. A friend gave me the wool, so it didn't cost me anything.

The washing instructions are very important. You ³_____ wash it in cold water, OK? And wash it by hand. You ⁴_____ put it in the washing machine. Never do that!

I'm really tired! I ⁵_____ do the washing-up now, but I really don't want to. I think I'll just go to bed now and do it in the morning.

Sarah

	mustn't	shall	(must)
1	Shall	Must	Shouldn't
2	have to	must	should
3	shall	must	have to
4	mustn't	shouldn't	don't
5	shall	shouldn't	should

2 Read the text. Choose a word from the box. Write the correct word next to numbers 1–5.

> ~~do~~   don't   has   have   must   mustn't
> shall   should   shouldn't   think

'I love playing the piano. I often perform at concerts. A lot of people ask me, '_Do_ you have to practise every day?' Well, I ¹_____ practise every day but I usually practise three or four times a week. I learnt to play the piano when I was a child. I ²_____ all children should learn to play a musical instrument. You ³_____ to work hard at first. But then it becomes more creative and you ⁴_____ have to think so much – you just 'feel' the music. Do you like classical music? ⁵_____ I play something for you now?'

Listening

3 ▶ R9.1 Listen and write.

MOUNTAIN HIKE
▶ Arrive at school _8.45 a.m._
1 **Clothes** wear light, _____ clothes
2 **Shoes** walking boots or _____
3 **In backpack** lunch, drink, _____ and a waterproof jacket
4 **What food?** Sandwiches, fruit, _____
5 **What drink?** _____

Speaking

4 Talk in pairs. Look at the pictures. What are the people saying? Use *mustn't*, *shall*, *have to*, *should* or *shouldn't*.

"You mustn't go in there!"

Units 16–17   95

Revision 4 Units 14–17

Reading and Writing

1 Look and read. Choose the correct words and write them on the lines.

mosquitoes   postcards   injection
sun cream   passport   ~~rucksack~~

▶ You can put lots of things in it. A customs officer might look inside it at the airport.
  rucksack

1 Are you going to travel to another country? You have to have this. _____

2 Are you going to travel to a hot country? A doctor might give you this before you go. _____

3 You can buy these at popular tourist places. You can write on them and send them to your friends. _____

4 You should use this in sunny places to protect your skin. _____

5 They might bite you. They can make you ill. They can fly. _____

2 Read the conversation. Match 1–5 with a–h. You don't have to use all the letters.

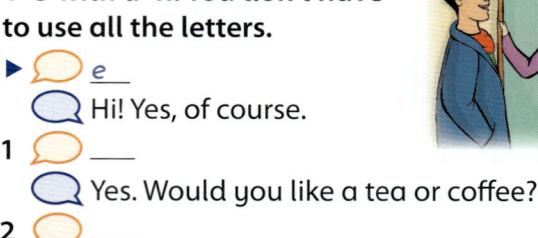

▶ 💬 _e_
  💬 Hi! Yes, of course.
1 💬 ___
  💬 Yes. Would you like a tea or coffee?
2 💬 ___
  💬 OK. What about a biscuit?
3 💬 ___
  💬 You can eat here, if you like.
4 💬 ___
  💬 Oh, that's a shame.
5 💬 ___
  💬 Yes, go ahead. It's in the kitchen.

a I have to have lunch at work today, unfortunately.
b Shall I put my coat here?
c May I use your phone for a quick call?
d Could I just have some water, please?
e ~~Hello. Can I come in?~~
f I might not sit down.
g No, thanks. I must go and have lunch soon.
h I can cook a meal for us.

3 Read the email. Choose the words and write them on the lines.

can't   couldn't   don't   might   ~~must~~
shall   shouldn't can   should

Dear Helen

I _must_ tell you about the new drama club at the Lighthouse Theatre. I love it! You ¹_____ have to be a good actor. You can choose from different games and activities. When I started at the club, I was shy and I ²_____ stand up and speak to the group. Now I can do it with no problems! You ³_____ come with me next time. ⁴_____ I send you the link to the website?

Jane

P.S. I'm not sure, but I ⁵_____ ask Elizabeth to come to us, too. What do you think?

96 Units 14–17

Listening

4 ▶ R10.1 Listen and write.

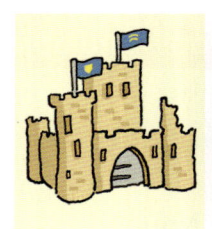

▶ Go everywhere in the castle? _yes_
1. Explore the castle park? _____
2. Explore Bayham forest in the morning? _____
3. Wear school uniform? _____
4. You can bring a _____
5. You must bring a _____

5 ▶ R10.2 Who does each object belong to? Listen and write a letter in each box.

▶ Alex's sister [c]
1. Alex's grandfather [ ] 
2. Alex [ ]
3. Alex's mum [ ]
4. Alex's dad [ ]
5. Alex's brother [ ]

Speaking

6 Work in pairs. Complete the table. Ask your partner questions to get the information you need. Use *Can you …?* and *Do you have to …?* and the prompts.

Sunny Vale High School

call a teacher / his or her first name	no
stand up / when a teacher comes in	yes
wear / a school uniform	yes
run / in the playground	yes
What subjects / have to do	maths and English
What sports / can / do	tennis, swimming

Your school

call a teacher / his or her first name	
stand up / when a teacher comes in	
wear / a school uniform	
run / in the playground	
What subjects / have to do	
What sports / can / do	

7 Work in different pairs. Ask your partner the questions from exercise 6.

Can you call the teacher by his or her first name at Sunny Vale High school?

No, you can't.

Can you call the teacher by his or her first name at your school?

Yes, you can.

Revision 4

18 Adjectives

I can recognize and use adjectives in sentences to describe people and objects.

What a beautiful picture! It's colourful and interesting.

It isn't beautiful! It's strange and ugly.

We use adjectives to describe nouns (things and people).
You're **crazy**!
That isn't a **beautiful** picture.

Adjectives stay the same with singular and plural nouns.
It's a **nice** colour.
They're **nice** colours.

We put an adjective before a noun.

	Adjective	Noun
I like	funny	films.
We ate a	big	breakfast.

We put an **adjective** after **be**:

	be	Adjective
It	's	red.
He	was	nice.

But when there is an article (**a**, **an** and **the**), the article goes between **be** and the adjective.

	be	Article	Adjective	Noun
It	's	a	red	bag.
He	was	a	nice	man.

The film was **good**.   It was a **good** film.

Sometimes the article changes from **a** to **an** or **an** to **a** when we use an adjective. When the adjective begins with a vowel we use **a**; when an adjective begins with a consonant we use **an**.

a → an	an → a
It's **a** book.	He's **an** engineer.
It's **a big** book.	He's **an English** engineer.
It's **an old** book.	He's **a French** engineer.

We also use adjectives after **become**, **get**, **seem** and verbs of sensation (**look**, **feel**, **taste**, **smell**, **sound**).
You **seem sad** today.   I'm **getting cold**.

For more information on verbs of sensation, see unit 7.

*1 Circle twelve more adjectives in the story.

Last week our teacher took us on a (fantastic) class trip. We took the train to the city centre to visit two big museums. In the morning we went to the Natural History Museum. We saw lots of old dinosaur skeletons and other interesting things. We had our lunch and a hot drink in a café. In the afternoon we went to the Science Museum. It was good too, but I was getting tired by this time. Unfortunately, the journey home was long. The train was late *and* it was slow. But we sang some traditional songs and told some funny stories, so time passed quickly.

2 Write the opposites.

~~hot~~ easy boring fast long late
dirty short modern safe heavy old

▶ cold _hot_
1 dangerous _____
2 short _____
3 clean _____
4 interesting _____
5 light _____
6 tall _____
7 early _____
8 difficult _____
9 slow _____
10 old _____
11 young _____

3 Look at the pictures and circle the correct adjective. Write phrases with the adjectives. Use the nouns in the box.

~~a football~~ a drink an egg a car a ring
an ice cream a TV show a door

▶ clean / (dirty)   _a dirty football_
1 hot / cold   _____
2 brown / blue   _____
3 fast / slow   _____
4 expensive / cheap   _____
5 big / small   _____
6 funny / boring   _____
7 open / closed   _____

4 **GAME** ▶ 18.1 Memory Game! Don't look at exercise 3. Listen. Are these sentences right or wrong? Correct the wrong sentences.

"The football was clean."

"That's wrong! The football was dirty."

5 ▶ 18.2 Listen and answer the questions about pronunciation. Then listen again and repeat.

1 Circle the stressed words in each sentence.
They were (old) (shoes).
She's got a red bag.
The meal was expensive.
It's a new watch.
She bought a white hat.
The sea will be cold.

2 Circle the words that we often stress.
nouns
pronouns
verbs
articles
auxiliary verbs (will, be)
adjectives

6 ▶ 18.3 Circle the correct answers. Then listen and check. Listen again and repeat.

▶ He **famous is** / **('s famous)**.
1 That's my **computer old** / **old computer**.
2 You **tired look** / **look tired**. Are you OK?
3 It's **an good** / **a good** idea.
4 Can I have the **red pen** / **pen red**, please?
5 We're going to **be late** / **late be**.
6 Those pizzas are **bigs** / **big**.
7 Come on! It's time to **ready get** / **get ready**!
8 This soup **tastes good** / **good tastes**.
9 She's **a beautiful girl** / **beautiful a girl**.
10 This is **an interesting** / **a interesting** story.

Unit 18   99

7 Rewrite the sentences so that the meaning stays the same.

▶ These are good books.
  These books are good.
▶ That lesson was interesting.
  That was an interesting lesson.

1 This is a heavy bag.

2 Those drinks were expensive.

3 This party will be good.

4 That's a strange photo.

5 That test was easy.

6 These are beautiful flowers.

7 This is a slow computer.

8 Those shoes are nice.

8 ▶ 18.4 Match the questions to the answers. Then listen and check.

▶ What does your best friend look like? _d_
1 How are you feeling? ___
2 What's your schoolbag like? ___
3 How was your weekend? ___
4 What's the weather like today? ___
5 What's your bedroom like? ___
6 What are your neighbours like? ___

a It was good, thanks.
b They're quiet but friendly.
c It's warm. It's cloudy.
d ~~She's tall. She's beautiful.~~
e It's small. It's got white walls.
f It's old. It's dirty. It's heavy.
g I'm happy. I'm hungry.

9 Work in pairs. Ask and answer the questions in exercise 8. Give your own answers.

What does your best friend look like?

He's short. He's got dark hair.

10 GAME Work in groups. Read the instructions and play the game.

Instructions
1 Choose a word card. Keep it secret.
2 Write down three adjectives to describe it.
3 Read your three adjectives to your group.
4 The first person to guess the card wins a point.
5 Play again.

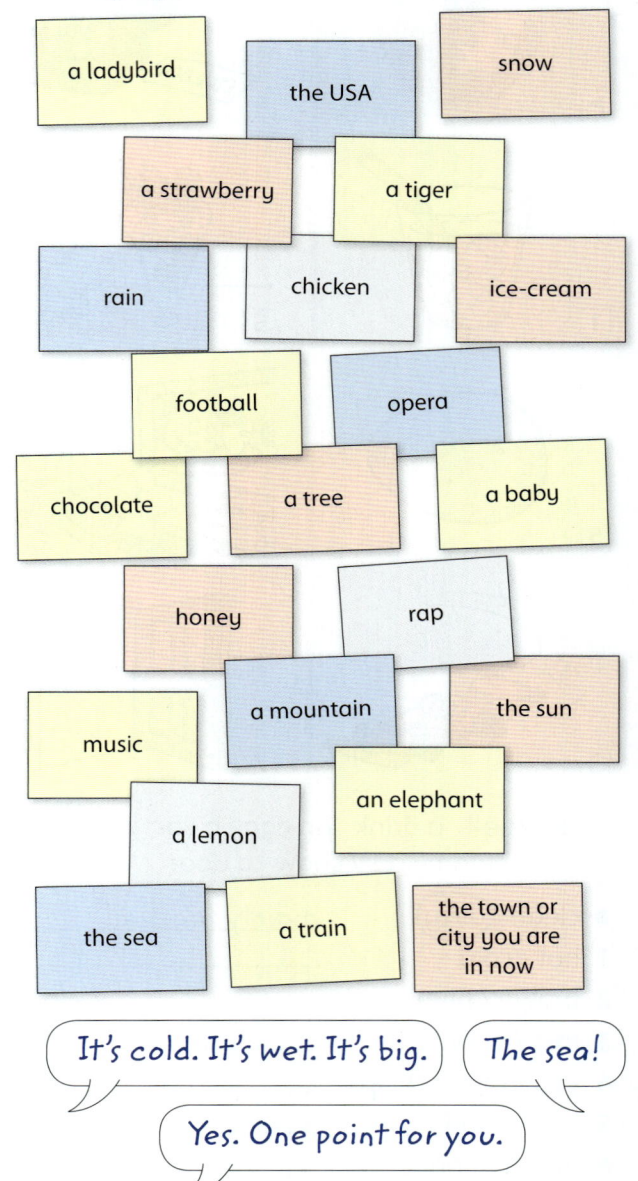

a ladybird · the USA · snow · a strawberry · a tiger · rain · chicken · ice-cream · football · opera · chocolate · a tree · a baby · honey · rap · a mountain · the sun · music · an elephant · a lemon · the sea · a train · the town or city you are in now

It's cold. It's wet. It's big. _The sea!_

Yes. One point for you.

100 Adjectives

Adjective order

When we use two or more adjectives, they usually follow this order:

Article	Size	Age	Colour	Nationality	Material	Noun
the	big		black			dog
an		old		French		chair
a			white		cotton	shirt
a		modern		Japanese		car
the	small				wooden	table

small · cheap · woollen · metal
leather · cotton · French · wooden

*11 Are the adjectives in the correct order? Tick ✓ the sentences that are correct. Change the order of the adjectives that are wrong.

▶ I'd like an old leather jacket. ✓
▶ We found a (metal small) box. _small metal_
1. I need a paper white bag. _____
2. They put everything in a big cardboard box. _____
3. Let's get some modern wooden furniture. _____
4. There were some small white mice. _____
5. He's a Spanish old actor. _____
6. Is that a new glass vase? _____
7. I'm wearing cotton blue socks. _____
8. He's got blue big eyes. _____
9. We watched an old Russian film. _____
10. I can't find my grey woollen jumper. _____
11. I'd like an American big car. _____
12. She's got black short hair. _____
13. Use the new white cups. _____

Unit 18 101

12 Complete the descriptions of the people and things. Use the adjectives in the box.

> big blue woollen green red Egyptian short metal paper black-and-white
> brown cotton old ~~small~~ ~~glass~~ long wooden German small white

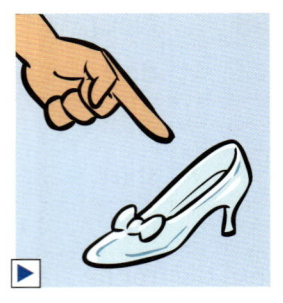

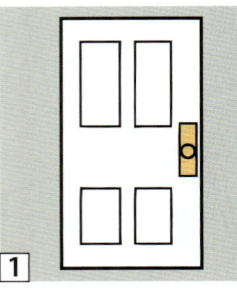

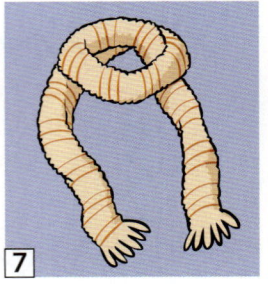

▶ It's a _small_ _glass_ shoe.
1 It's a _____ _____ door.
2 They're _____ _____ sheets.
3 They're _____ _____ robots.
4 It's an _____ _____ film.
5 She's got _____ _____ hair.
6 They're _____ _____ cups.
7 It's a _____ _____ scarf.
8 He's got _____ _____ eyes.
9 It's a _____ _____ car.

13 GAME Work in pairs. Look at the pictures in exercise 12 but cover the adjectives and sentences. How many descriptions can you remember?

14 Write about each of the topics below.

An important possession
Write about its age, size, colour and material.
Where does it come from?
Why is it important to you?

A special person
What does he / she look like?
Write about his / her hair and eyes.
What is he / she like?
Write about his / her character and personality.

A SPECIAL POSSESSION
I have an old ring. It's small and it isn't beautiful but it's important to me. It was …

Self-evaluation Rate your progress.

102 Adjectives

19 Adverbs

I can recognize and use adverbs of manner, time and frequency.

Types of adverbs and adverbs of manner

I've already finished.
You eat quickly.
You always say that!

Already, quickly, and **always** are different kinds of adverbs. They give information about time, manner and frequency.

Adjectives describe nouns (things and people).
*She has a **quiet** voice.*
*It's a **noisy** dog.*
They often answer questions with **What … ?**

WOOF
Be quiet!

Adverbs of manner describe how people do things.
*She speaks **quietly**.* *The dog barks **noisily**.*
They often answer questions with **How … ?**

Most adjectives change to adverbs of manner like this.

Most regular adjectives	Adjectives ending in -y	Adjectives ending in -ble
+ **ly**	-i**ly**	-**bly**
nice → nice**ly**	angry → angr**ily**	comfortable → comforta**bly**

There are some irregular adverbs of manner.
good → **well**
He's a good swimmer. → He swims **well**.
fast → **fast**
She's a fast runner. → She runs **fast**.
hard → **hard**
They're hard workers. → They work **hard**.

We usually use adverbs after verbs.
*She sings **beautifully**.*

However, we use adjectives after the verbs **be**, **seem**, **become**, **get**, **look**, **feel**, **taste**, **smell** and **sound**.
*Her voice sounds **beautiful**.*
*You'll get **hungry**.*

---

*1 Change the adverbs into adjectives.

▶ nicely *nice*   3 easily _____
1 quickly _____   4 hard _____
2 well _____   5 beautifully _____

*2 Circle the correct form.

▶ You walk slow /(slowly)!
1 You seem **sad** / **sadly** today.
2 She plays volleyball **good** / **well**.
3 Are you **angry** / **angrily** with me?
4 I can speak French, but **bad** / **badly**!
5 I can **easy** / **easily** finish this book today.
6 Are you sitting **comfortable** / **comfortably**?
7 Read it **careful** / **carefully**.
8 My feet are getting **cold** / **coldly**.

*3 ▶ 19.1 Listen and write the correct adverb. Use the adjectives below.

| noisy ~~careful~~ clear fast |
| happy polite quiet slow |

▶ He's working *carefully*_____.
1 She's speaking _____.
2 He's riding his bike very _____.
3 She's speaking _____.
4 He's working _____.
5 They're singing very _____.
6 He's asking _____.
7 She's walking _____.

Unit 19   103

4 ▶ **19.2** Listen. Which animals are the people talking about? Write the number.

parrots  ___   hummingbirds ___

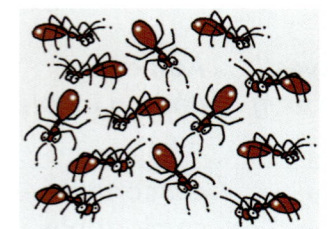

ants  ___   tortoises ___

cheetahs  ___   dogs _1_

5 ▶ **19.3** Choose a verb and an adverb for each animal. Listen again to check.

Verbs
~~see, hear and smell~~   move   speak
run   communicate   shine

Adverbs
clearly   funnily   slowly   brightly
~~very well~~   fast

1 Dogs _see, hear and smell_ _very well_.
2 Ants _____ _____.
3 Parrots _____ _____.
4 Tortoises _____ _____.
5 Cheetahs _____ _____.
6 Hummingbirds _____ _____.

6 Write six sentences using words and phrases from below. Work in small groups. Read your sentences to your group. Are any of your sentences the same?

My best friend dances very badly.
My sister works hard.

I
my sister
my best friend
my brother

can run
can paint   can ski
walks   work(s)   eat(s)
cook(s)   sing(s)   dance(s)
read(s)   draw(s)   people
play(s)
golf / football / chess
speak(s)
English / French /
Chinese / Arabic

well   quickly
hard   slowly   very
badly   easily
beautifully   clearly
realistically

7 **GAME** Work in groups. Act an action from the box with an adverb from the box. Can your friends guess the adverb?

Actions
say 'hello'   write your name   clap your hands
close your book   ask for a dictionary
stand up and sit down again

Adverbs of manner
quickly   slowly   quietly   funnily   nicely
angrily   happily   clearly

Are you writing your name slowly?

Yes, I am.

104   Adverbs

Adverbs of frequency

We use adverbs of frequency to say how often something happens.

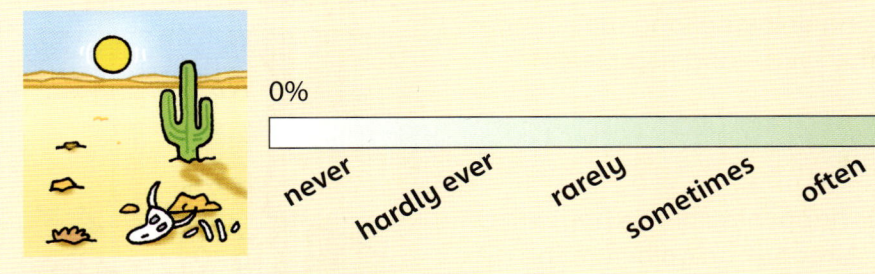

0% never, hardly ever, rarely, sometimes, often, usually, always 100%

It **never** rains here.

It **always** rains here.

We often use these adverbs of frequency with the present simple.
We **rarely** go to the cinema.
Jane **sometimes** wears glasses.

We use **ever** with the present simple and present perfect to ask about habits and experiences.
Do you **ever** go running?
Have you **ever** read this book?

We can also use **often** and **never** with the present perfect when we talk about experiences.
I've **often** thought about it.
They've **never** been here.

We put the adverb before main verbs.
Robert **hardly ever** walks to school.
She **always** wakes up early.

We put the adverb after **be** and auxiliary verbs like **don't**, **can** and **have**.
You're **always** hungry!
He can **usually** do it.
She doesn't **often** sit there.

We also use adverbial expressions to talk about frequency. These expressions go at the end of the sentence.

present simple + **every day, on Wednesdays**
She phones me **every day**.
They meet **on Fridays**.

present perfect + **once, twice, a few times**
He's visited us **twice**.
I've been to Paris **a few times**.

*8 Put the words in brackets in the correct place in these sentences.
▶ Carla has a big breakfast. (usually) — *usually*
1 You phone me. (hardly ever)
2 He's been to hospital. (a few times)
3 The train's late. (often)
4 Have you climbed a tree? (ever)
5 My grandma's very kind. (always)
6 Do you have bad dreams? (ever)
7 How do you drink milk? (often)
8 There's anybody in that café. (rarely)

*9 🎵 ▶ 19.4 Read and ask your partner the questions. Listen and repeat. Say the chant with a partner.

Do you always brush your teeth?
Do you? Do you?
Yes, I always brush my teeth. Of course I do!
Do you ever bite your nails? Do you? Do you?
Well, I sometimes bite my nails.
I sometimes do that.
Are you ever late for school? Are you? Are you?
No, I'm never late for school. Of course I'm not.
Do you always make your bed?
Do you? Do you?
Yes, I always make my bed …
Well, I usually make my bed …
Well, I often make my bed …
but sometimes I forget!

Unit 19 105

Adverbs of time: **still**, **yet**, **already**

We use **still**, **yet** and **already** to show how we feel about events in time.

We use **still** to show that something is taking or lasts a long time. It goes after auxiliary verbs and **be**, but before main verbs and negative auxiliaries or modals (e.g. **haven't**, **can't**).
Lily **still** hasn't done her homework.
I'm **still** waiting for the bus.

We use **already** to show that something is happening or has happened more quickly than is normal or expected. **Already** can go before the main verb or at the end of the sentence.
I've **already** cleaned the bathroom.
I've cleaned the bathroom **already**.

We use **yet** at the end of questions and negatives to emphasize 'up to now'.
Do you know the answer **yet**? No, not **yet**.
She hasn't written the letter **yet**.

We can use **still**, **yet** and **already** with the present simple, present continuous and present perfect.

Are you a teenager yet?
No. I'm still 12.
I'm 13. I'm already a teenager.

10 Choose the correct answers.
▶ They're not ready **still** / **yet**.
1 Wait! I **already** / **still** can't find my bag.
2 Has Julia finished eating **yet** / **still**?
3 I don't believe it! You **still** / **yet** haven't finished that book!
4 What do you want for lunch?
   Erm … I've **still** / **already** had lunch!
5 Has it stopped raining?
   No, not **already** / **yet**.
6 We've got Mr Wood for maths again this year.
   Do you **still** / **already** have Mr Wood? We've got a different teacher this year.

11 Complete each sentence with *still*, *yet* or *already*.
▶ I've had lunch but I'm _still_ hungry!
1 Have you phoned Billy _____?
2 I've had a holiday but I'm _____ thinking about my next holiday!
3 I haven't met your new friends _____.
4 Wow! You've _____ done your homework. That was quick!
5 Pat got in the bath at seven o'clock and he's _____ there now.
6 That film was scary! I'm _____ thinking about it!

12 Look at the events in the box. Put a tick in the column that's true for you, then write sentences with *still*, *already* or *not yet*. Use the present simple, the present continuous or the present perfect.

Life events	still	already	not yet
be at school			
be a teenager			
get my own phone			
visit a foreign country			
live with my family			
learn to swim			
learn to drive			
choose my career			
meet my husband / wife			

I'm still at school. I'm already a teenager. I haven't got my own phone yet.

13 Work in small groups. Compare your answers.

I'm still at school. *Me too.*
I haven't chosen my career yet.
That's the same for me.

14 Are the adverbs in the correct place? Tick ✓ the sentences that are correct. Correct the sentences that are wrong.

▶ Have you yet told her? ✗
  <u>Have you told her yet?</u>

1 She can well speak French.

2 The train hasn't left yet.

3 He slowly drives.

4 I have sometimes eggs for breakfast.

5 I've drunk all my water but I'm still thirsty.

6 She's already said 'goodbye' six times!

7 I don't watch usually the news on TV.

15 How well do you know your group? Complete the sentences with the names of people in your group.

▶ <u>Olly</u> can speak English well.
1 _____ is usually happy.
2 _____ has never arrived late for school.
3 _____ can already ride a motorbike.
4 _____ always speaks politely to the teacher.
5 _____ is sometimes late for school.
6 _____ draws well.
7 _____ hasn't eaten any fruit yet today.
8 _____ can swim fast.
9 _____ often makes people laugh.
10 _____ speaks quickly.
11 _____ has been abroad a few times.
12 _____ never sits quietly!

16 Work in groups. Read your sentences. Do your friends think your ideas are right?

Olly can speak English well.
That's true.
I agree!
But he speaks English slowly.
That's not a problem.
He speaks clearly.

Self-evaluation Rate your progress.

	😊	😊😊	😊😊😊
1			
2			
3			
4			
5			
6			
7			
8			
9			
10			
11			
12			
13			
14			
15			
16			

20 Comparative and superlative adjectives

I can recognize and use comparative adjectives and superlative adjectives.

Comparative adjectives

We use comparative adjectives when we compare two people, places, animals or objects.
Elephants are **taller** than horses.
Giraffes are **taller** than elephants.

Adjectives change to comparative adjectives like this.

Short adjectives: + er / + r

Adjective	Comparative adjective
tall	tall**er**
big*	big**ger**
nice	nic**er**

* Double the final consonant in adjectives that end vowel + consonant: big → **bigger**

Adjectives ending with -y

Adjective	Comparative adjective
hungry	hungr**ier**
friendly	friendl**ier**

Long adjectives (two or more syllables)

Adjective	Comparative adjective
difficult	**more** difficult
intelligent	**more** intelligent

Irregular adjectives

Adjective	Comparative adjective
good	better
bad	worse

Giraffes are taller than elephants.

Giraffes are the tallest animals in Africa.

We can use comparative adjectives after **be**, **look**, **get** and **feel**.

We usually use **than** after comparative adjectives.
They're **more expensive than** apples.

We can sometimes use a comparative adjective on its own to describe a change.
The weather's getting **colder**. (= colder than it was before)
I feel **better** now. (= better than I felt yesterday)

*1 Write the comparative form of these adjectives.

▶ fast → *faster*
1 long → _____
2 thin → _____
3 special → _____
4 easy → _____
5 slow → _____
6 beautiful → _____
7 funny → _____
8 strong → _____
9 small → _____
10 good → _____
11 nice → _____
12 pretty → _____
13 red → _____

2 ▶ **20.1** Write these sentences in the correct order. Listen and check, then listen and repeat.

▶ bikes / than / cars / faster / are
  Cars are faster than bikes.

1 worse / the / getting / weather's
  _____

2 gold / paper / more / is / than / expensive
  _____

3 are / stronger / you / me / than
  _____

4 better / getting / English / my / is
  _____

5 giraffes / taller / lions / are / than
  _____

6 than / heavier / stone / wood / is
  _____

7 looks / that / comfortable / bed / more
  _____

8 more / your / mine / than / book / interesting / looks
  _____

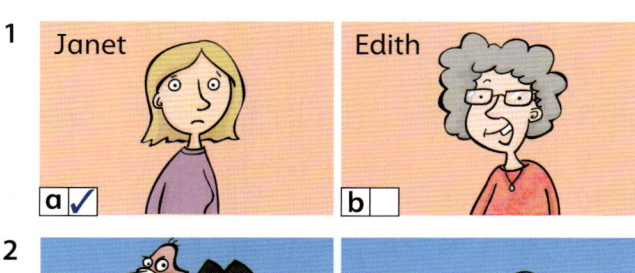

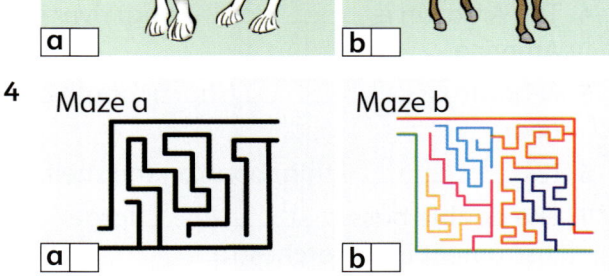

3 ▶ **20.2** Listen to the questions and tick ✓ the correct picture.

1 Janet [a ✓]   Edith [b ☐]
2 [a ☐]   [b ☐]
3 [a ☐]   [b ☐]
4 Maze a [a ☐]   Maze b [b ☐]

4 Write more sentences about the pictures in exercise 3 with *be* or *look* + a comparative adjective. Use the adjectives in the box.

> colourful safe interesting fast noisy
> quiet friendly slow happy sad
> dangerous young

Janet is younger than Edith.
Edith looks happier than Janet.

5 Complete the questions with the comparative form of the adjective in brackets and *than*.

▶ Are your shoes <u>cleaner than</u> (clean) my shoes?

1 Are you _____ (old) me?
2 Is your chair _____ (comfortable) mine?
3 Are your hands _____ (big) mine?
4 Is your bag _____ (heavy) my bag?
5 Are films _____ (interesting) books?
6 Are computers _____ (intelligent) people?
7 Were people in the past _____ (happy) people today?
8 Is English _____ (complicated) other languages?
9 Is the countryside _____ (safe) the city?
10 Are boys (good) _____ girls at sport?

6 Ask and answer the questions in exercise 5 with a partner.

> Are your shoes cleaner than my shoes?

> I don't know. Let's compare. No, your shoes are cleaner than my shoes!

Unit 20 **109**

Superlative adjectives

We use superlative adjectives when we compare a person, animal, place or thing with all of the group they are in.
*That giraffe is **the tallest** animal in the zoo.*
*Giraffes are **the tallest** animals in the world.*

Adjectives change to superlative adjectives like this.

Short adjectives

Adjective	Superlative adjective
young	the youngest
rich	the richest
sad	the saddest*

* Double the final consonant in adjectives that end vowel + consonant:
sad → **the saddest**, wet → **the wettest**

Adjectives ending with -y

Adjective	Superlative adjective
funny	the funniest
happy	the happiest

Long adjectives (two or more syllables)

Adjective	Superlative adjective
comfortable	the most comfortable
delicious	the most delicious

Irregular adjectives

Adjective	Superlative adjective
good	the best
bad	the worst

We always use **the** before superlative adjectives.
*Ronny's **the funniest** person in the class.*

After superlative adjectives we usually use **in** or **on** before the name of a place.
*It's **the biggest** lake **in** Europe.*
*It's **the most dangerous** place **on** Earth.*

*7 **Comparative or superlative? Circle the correct form.**
▶ What's **stronger** / (**the strongest**) bone in the human body?
1 Is a lion **bigger** / **biggest** than a tiger?
2 What's **hotter** / **the hottest** place in the world?
3 Who's **younger** / **the youngest** person in this class?
4 Excuse me, where's **nearer** / **the nearest** post office?
5 This computer is getting **slower** / **the slowest**.
6 You're getting **taller** / **the tallest**!
7 Your hair is **longer** / **the longest** than mine.
8 He's **more** / **the most** intelligent person in my family.

*8 ▶ 20.3 **Write the superlative form of these adjectives. Listen and repeat.**
▶ nicest → _the nicest_
1 long → _____
2 good → _____
3 sad → _____
4 tasty → _____
5 difficult → _____
6 noisy → _____
7 safe → _____
8 bad → _____
9 dry → _____
10 colourful → _____
11 funny → _____
12 thin → _____

*9 **Complete the sentences.**
▶ My grandma is _the oldest_ person in my family.
1 He's _____ (young) musician in the band.
2 That's _____ (comfortable) chair in the room.
3 She's _____ (tall) player in the team.
4 The Amazon is _____ (long) river in South America.
5 February is _____ (short) month of the year.
6 It's _____ (thin) book on the shelf.
7 The double bass is _____ (large) instrument in the orchestra.

110 Comparative and superlative adjectives

10 Write the questions with superlative adjectives. Then use the questions to interview a partner.

Who's the youngest person in your family?

My cousin Frank. He's six months old.

▶ Who / young / person / your family?
   Who's the youngest person in your family?
1 What / beautiful / place / in this country?
2 What / bad / day of the week for you?
3 What / good / part of the day for you?
4 Where / near / supermarket?
5 Who / tall / person / in this class?
6 Who / clever / person / in your family?
7 Who / good / singer / in the world?
8 What / old / area / in this town?
9 What / important / thing / in your life?
10 Who / important / person / in your life?
11 What / interesting / book / on your bookshelf?
12 What / expensive / thing / in your room?

11 Which is the best gift for each person? Talk in pairs, using the words below. Then compare your choices with other pairs.

expensive fun cheap safe beautiful
useful interesting nice special

Peter  — some grapes  some flowers  a puzzle book  some chocolates

Your aunt 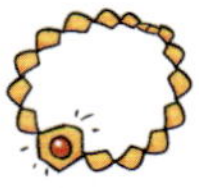 — a necklace  some flowers  a magazine  a pair of socks

Milly 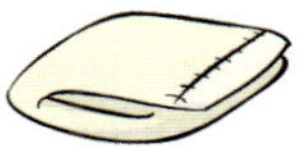 — a blanket  a toy rabbit  a camera  some earrings

Your teacher  — a box of chocolates  a plant  a book  a pen

Which is the best present for Peter?

Grapes are nice, but the puzzle book is more interesting.

Yes, I think the puzzle book is the best present.

Unit 20 111

12 Complete 1–8 with the superlative forms of the adjectives. Do not answer the questions yet.

General knowledge quiz

1 <u>The deepest</u> (deep) ocean on Earth is:
   A ☐ the Atlantic Ocean
   B ☑ the Pacific Ocean
   C ☐ the Indian Ocean

2 _____ (dry) desert on Earth is:
   A ☐ the Gobi Desert, China
   B ☐ the Sahara Desert, Egypt
   C ☐ the Atacama Desert, Chile

3 Scientists believe _____ (old) living species of animal in the world is a kind of:
   A ☐ insect   B ☐ crab   C ☐ bird

4 _____ (heavy) animal in the world is:
   A ☐ the blue whale
   B ☐ the saltwater crocodile
   C ☐ the hippopotamus

5 _____ (large) cut diamond in the world is:
   A ☐ the Cullinan 1
   B ☐ the Koh-i-Noor
   C ☐ the Millennium Star

6 _____ (long) snake in the world is:
   A ☐ the python
   B ☐ the cobra
   C ☐ the anaconda

7 For humans, _____ (dangerous) animals in the world are:
   A ☐ snakes
   B ☐ sharks
   C ☐ bears

8 _____ (noisy) animal on land is a kind of:
   A ☐ wolf
   B ☐ elephant
   C ☐ monkey

13 **GAME** Work in teams. Can you guess the answers to the questions in the quiz?

14 ▶ 20.4 Now listen to the answers to the quiz. How many correct answers did your team get?

Self-evaluation Rate your progress.

	☺	☺☺	☺☺☺
1			
2			
3			
4			
5			
6			
7			
8			
9			
10			
11			
12			
13			
14			

112 Comparative and superlative adjectives

Revision 5   Units 18–20

Reading and writing

1 Look and read. Choose the correct words and write them on the lines.

> hot air balloon   ~~car~~   motorbike
> rocket   train   walking

▶ You must drive this slowly in town but you can drive it fast on the motorway. _car_

1 It's faster than a plane. _____
2 This is the most peaceful way to travel in the air. _____
3 Lots of people do this every day. It's the oldest way of moving about. _____
4 It's the longest form of transport. It's got a lot of wheels. _____
5 It's got two wheels. It's bigger and faster than a bicycle. _____

2 Read the text. Circle the correct answers.

My great aunt Emily is **than** / **(the)** / **a** oldest person ¹ **in** / **of** / **at** my family. She's ninety-five years old but she is ² **already** / **yet** / **still** fit and well. She's very ³ **calmly** / **calm** / **calmly**. She sleeps ⁴ **good** / **well** / **often** at night. And she seems happier ⁵ **that** / **than** / **of** all my other family and friends.

So what's great aunt Emily's secret? She eats very ⁶ **health** / **healthy** / **healthily**. She isn't a vegetarian but she hardly ⁷ **never** / **ever** / **rarely** eats meat. She eats lots of rice and vegetables and she eats ⁸ **fresh** / **fresher** / **freshly** fish four times a week. Also, she gets up at 5.30 a.m. every day. She ⁹ **ever** / **always** / **every** says, 'The morning is the best part ¹⁰ **at** / **in** / **of** the day.'

3 Read the text. Choose the correct words from the box and write them next to 1–9.

> already   ~~oldest~~   bigger   biggest
> in   more   most   of   rarely   yet

Lake Baikal and Olkhon Island

Lake Baikal in Russia is the _oldest_ lake in the world. It is also the world's ¹_____ lake. With an area of 730 km², Olkhon Island is ²_____ than any other island ³_____ Lake Baikal. It's a beautiful place and it ⁴_____ rains there. ⁵_____ people on Olkhon are fishermen or farmers. But these days tourism is becoming a ⁶_____ important part ⁷_____ the economy on Olkhon and all around the lake. A tourist organisation called the Great Baikal Trail is building a 1,800 km footpath around the lake. They haven't finished the path ⁸_____, but walkers can ⁹_____ use some parts of it.

Listening

4 ▶ **R11.1** Listen and draw lines.

Helen   Charlie   Louise

Robert   Isabel   Andy

5 ▶ **R11.2** Listen and write. There is one example.

STUDY HABITS

▶ **Read?** *quickly*

1 **Write?** slowly and _____
2 **At home?** No, because it's _____ and noisy
3 **At the library?** Yes, at the town library because it's bigger and _____ than the school library
4 **Study and listen to music?** _____
5 **Review notes?** _____ a month

Speaking

6 Work in pairs. Student A look at the information below. Student B turn to page 156. Complete the table. Ask your partner questions to get the information you need. Use the prompts.

The smallest bird in the world

Name	The Bee Hummingbird
Bigger than a bee?	yes, a little
Bigger than a large spider?	no
Colour	blue, red and green
Male bird or female bird bigger?	female
How often / male sit on the eggs?	never

The biggest flower in the world

Name	The Rafflesia
Heavier than a one-year-old child?	
Bigger than a large bicycle wheel?	
Colour	
Smell	
How often / it / produce a flower?	

What's the smallest bird in the world?

The Bee Hummingbird.

What's the biggest flower in the world?

The Rafflesia.

114   Units 18–20

21 Prepositions of place

I can recognize and use **in**, **on**, **at** and other prepositions of place to talk about location and position.

In, on and at

When we talk about place we often use the prepositions **in**, **on** and **at**.

We use **in** with three-dimensional spaces like rooms, houses, bags, cities and countries.

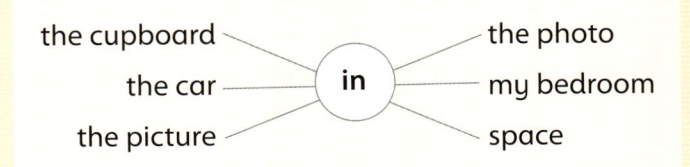

the cupboard — the photo
the car — **in** — my bedroom
the picture — space

The satellite is **in** space.
The hat is **in** a box **in** the cupboard **in** my bedroom.

We also use **in** with pictures and photos.
There are two tigers **in** the picture.
Jane's **in** this photo.

We use **on** with two-dimensional areas like walls, desks, maps and floors.

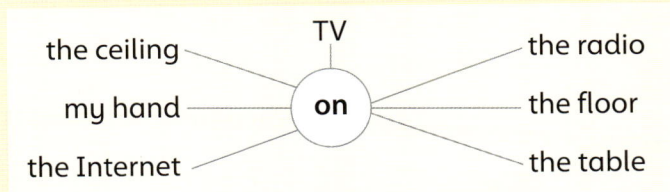

the ceiling — TV — the radio
my hand — **on** — the floor
the Internet — the table

There's a spider **on** the ceiling!
Put the boxes **on** the floor.

We also use **on** with the radio, TV and the Internet.
My brother was **on** TV yesterday.
I read about it **on** the Internet.

Where's Andorra?
Go and look **on** the Internet.
Where's the computer?
It's **under** the newspaper.
Where's the newspaper?
It's **on** the table! Look! It's **in front of** you!

We use **at** to show where things happen:

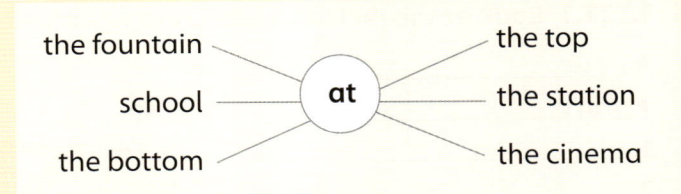

the fountain — the top
school — **at** — the station
the bottom — the cinema

Let's meet **at** the station.
Where's Tommy? He's **at** school.

We also use **at** with the top and the bottom.
There's a tree **at** the top of the hill.
Your shoes are **at** the bottom of the stairs.

*1 Circle the correct preposition.

▶ Leave your books **on** / at the table.
1 You've got paint **in** / **on** your arms!
2 There's some milk **in** / **at** the fridge.
3 He works **at** / **on** the new university.
4 It was very dark **in** / **on** the forest.
5 They live **on** / **in** Brazil.
6 Don't put your bag **on** / **at** the ground! It's wet!
7 Kelly's **on** / **at** school.
8 Are you **in** / **on** this photo?
9 I'll see you **in** / **at** the bus stop at eight o'clock.
10 Let's sit **on** / **at** the grass.
11 Room 3 is **at** / **on** the top of the building.
12 There's some writing **at** / **on** the ceiling.

Unit 21 115

2 Look and write *in*, *on* or *at*.

▶ They're _at_ the beach.
1 She's _____ the car.
2 It's _____ the car.
3 They're _____ the bus stop.
4 It's _____ the painting.
5 It's _____ the painting.
6 He's _____ the newspaper.
7 They're _____ a tennis match.
8 She's _____ home.

3 ▶ 21.1 Look at the picture. Listen and write 'true' or 'false'. Correct the false sentences.

▶ _True_
▶ _False_
1 _____
2 _____
3 _____
4 _____
5 _____
6 _____
7 _____
8 _____

4 Complete the questions with *in*, *on* or *at*. Then use the questions to interview a partner.

▶ Have you got anything _in_ your pockets?
1 Do you ever write _____ your hands?
2 Have you got a T-shirt with a picture _____ it? What's the picture?
3 Who in your family is _____ work at the moment?
4 When were you last _____ the cinema or theatre?
5 What's _____ your bag?
6 Do you listen to music _____ your bedroom?
7 Have you ever been _____ TV?
8 When you're _____ home where do you play? Where do you do your homework? Where do you eat breakfast?
9 Do any of your friends or family members live _____ Australia?
10 Is anyone in your family _____ university?

Have you got anything in your pockets?

Yes, I've got some money and a tissue.

116 Prepositions of place

Other prepositions of place

Like **in** and **on**, these other prepositions of place describe an object's location in relationship to another object.

It's **in front of** the sun.

It's **behind** the tree.

It's **above** the balloon.
(at a higher level)

It's **below** the bird.
(at a lower level)

It's **near** the house.

It's **between** the books and the photo.

It's **next to** the tennis racket.

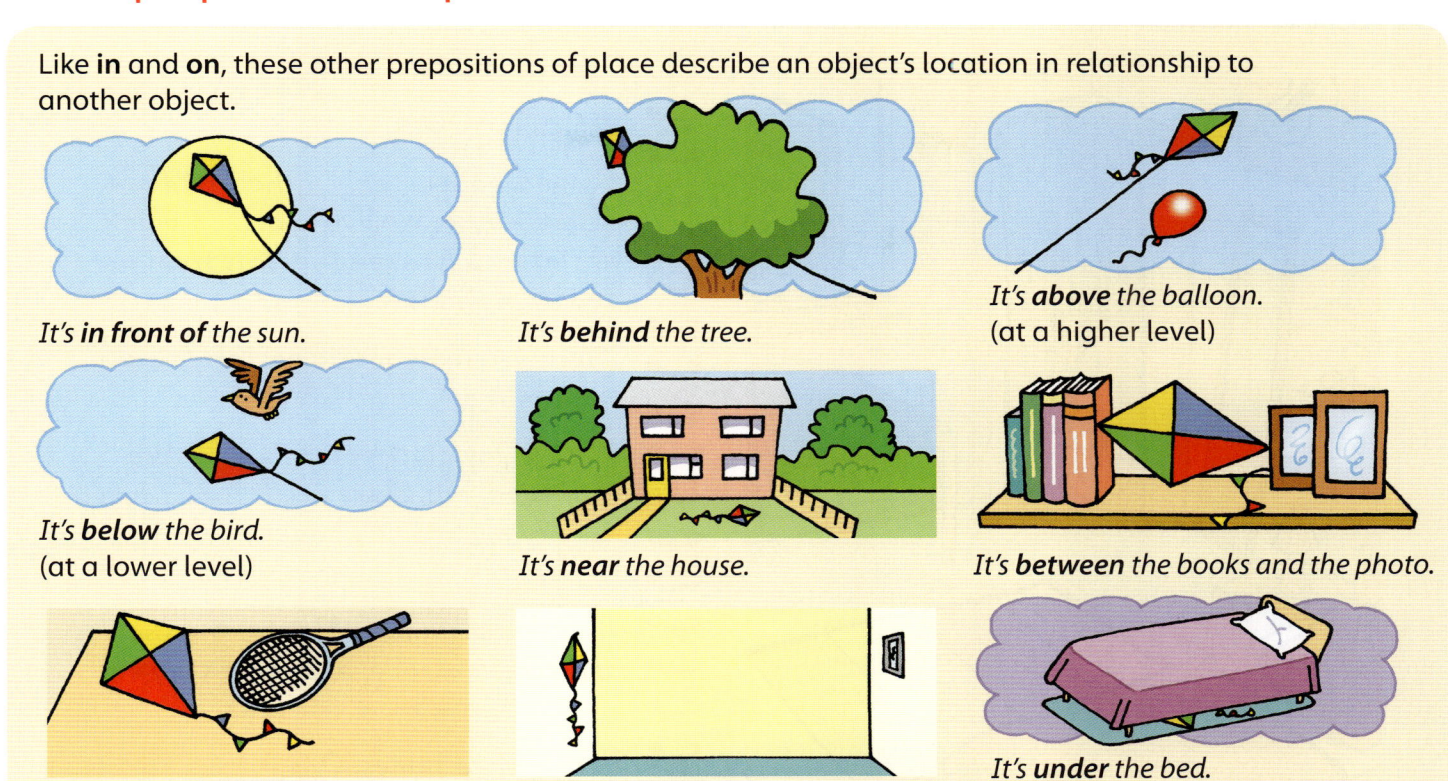

It's **opposite** the photo.

It's **under** the bed.
(covered by)

5 ▶ 21.2 Listen and tick ✓ the correct picture.

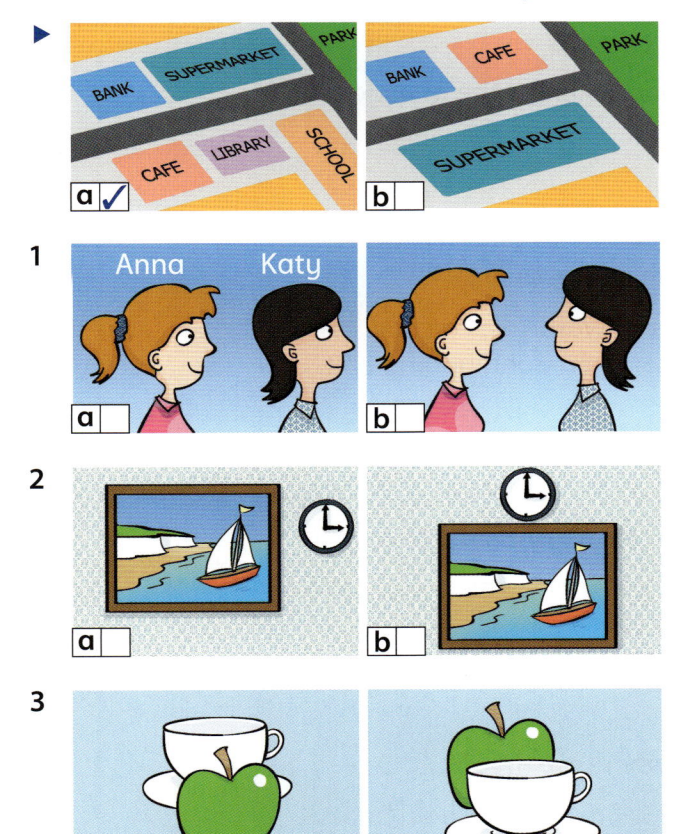

▶ a ✓ b

1 Anna Katy — a b
2 a b
3 a b

6 Circle the correct preposition.

▶ What's that **above** / (**behind**) / **below** your back? Show me!

1 Carrots grow **near** / **under** / **behind** the ground so you can't see them.
2 There's a big tree **behind** / **below** / **between** the school.
3 We live on the second floor. Mr Cox lives **next to** / **above** / **below** us, on the first floor.
4 I stood **near** / **below** / **opposite** the fire and it was hot.
5 Stand **behind** / **between** / **in front of** the tower. I'll take a photo of you.
6 Can I sit **opposite** / **next to** / **behind** you at the cinema?
7 Someone's coming! Quick! Hide **behind** / **under** / **above** that wall!
8 I can't see the TV! You're standing **next to** / **behind** / **in front of** it!

Unit 21 117

7 Look and read. Add the missing prepositions.

behind   between   in   in front of   next to   ~~on~~   on   on   opposite   under

MY BEDROOM

My bedroom is __on__ the first floor of the house. We live ¹_____ a block of flats – I can see the flats from my bedroom window.

There are some music posters ²_____ the wall.

Most of my clothes are ³_____ the wardrobe, but there are lots of shoes ⁴_____ my bed. My books and other things are ⁵_____ the shelves.

There's a big mirror ⁶_____ the shelves and the wardrobe, and some stickers ⁷_____ the mirror.

I've got two tables. One is ⁸_____ the window and the other is ⁹_____ my bed.

The radiator keeps the room warm. It's ¹⁰_____ the table.

8 Write about your bedroom and your classroom. Answer the questions.

My bedroom
1 Where is your bedroom in your house or flat?
2 What's above and below it?
3 Do you have these things in your bedroom? If so, where are they?

a clock   posters   photos   a lamp   books   shelves   a wardrobe   a chair   clothes   shoes   a rug   a mirror   a table   a radiator or air-conditioning unit

MY BEDROOM

My bedroom is at the top of the house. Our kitchen is below it. The neighbour's kitchen is above it. My bed is next to the window and there is …

My classroom
1 Where is your classroom in the school?
2 What's above and below it?
3 Where do you sit in the classroom?
4 Do you have these things in your classroom? If so, where are they?

notices   signs   charts   a clock   shelves   pictures   a fire extinguisher   books   a bin   a computer   rubbish   a radiator or air-conditioning unit

Prepositions of place

9 GAME Work in pairs. Describe and draw. Your pictures should match.

1 **Student A** Draw the objects in the first row on picture 1, then describe your picture to student B. Now listen to student B and draw the objects in the second row.

2 **Student B** Listen to student A and draw the objects in the first row on picture 2. Now draw the objects in the second row and describe your picture to student A.

The box is next to the tree and the diamond is in the box.

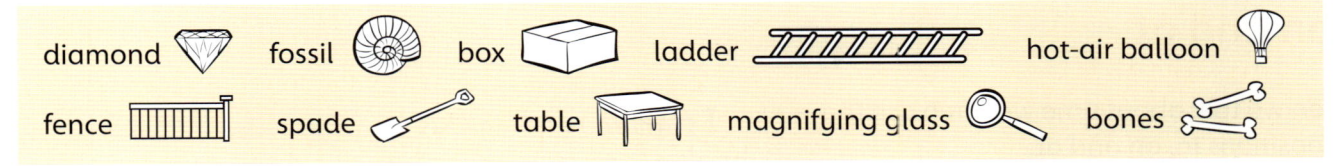

diamond   fossil   box   ladder   hot-air balloon
fence   spade   table   magnifying glass   bones

Student A

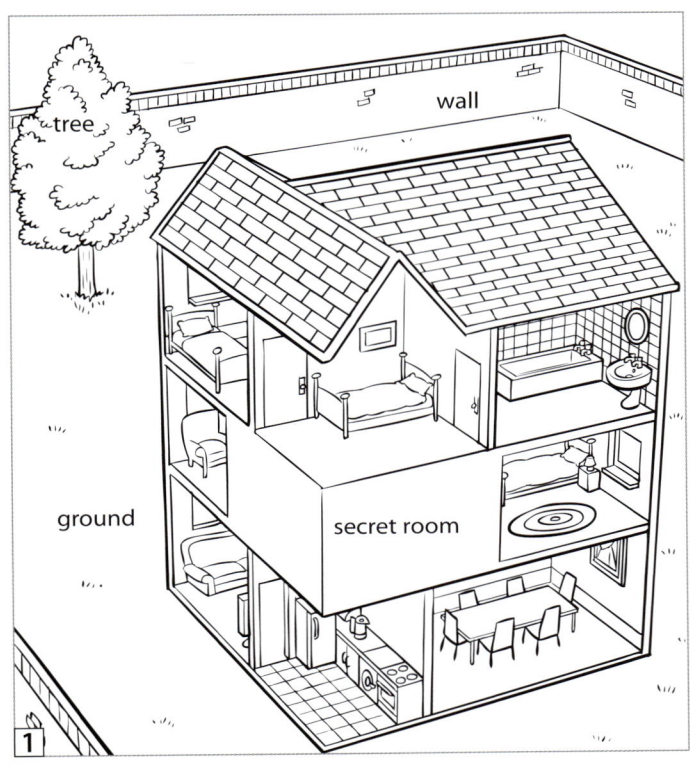

Student B

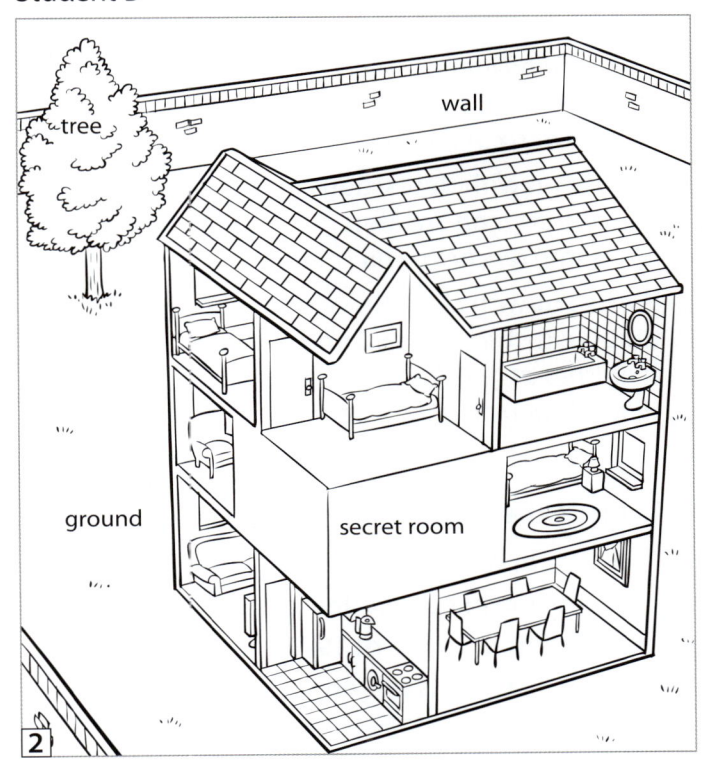

10 Talk in small groups. Where are these things in your home?

a clock   posters   photos   a lamp   books
shelves   a wardrobe   a chair   clothes
shoes   a rug   a mirror   a table   a radiator
or air-conditioning unit

Where is your clock?

It's on the wall.

Where are your posters?

I haven't got posters!

Self-evaluation Rate your progress.

	😊	😊😊	😊😊😊
1			
2			
3			
4			
5			
6			
7			
8			
9			
10			

Unit 21   119

22 Prepositions of time

I can recognize and use prepositions of time.

In, on and at

When we talk about time we often use the prepositions **in**, **on** and **at**.

We use **in** with years, seasons, months and parts of the day.
We go skiing **in** the winter.
He's going to the USA **in** June.
I get up **at** six **in** the morning.

We use **on** with dates, days and parts of days.
The concert is **on** 3rd May.
Mr Ashton teaches us **on** Fridays.

We use **at** with clock times and other regular times (e.g. the weekend and traditional festivals).
It finishes **at** ten o'clock **at** night.
What do you do **at** New Year?

I started reading this book at ten o'clock in the morning on 14th August.

At ten o'clock this morning, you mean?

No, at ten o'clock in the morning on 14th August last year!

*1 Circle the correct preposition.

▶ We came home in /(at) lunchtime.
1 See you **in** / **on** Wednesday!
2 He was born **in** / **at** 1972.
3 The film starts **at** / **on** six o'clock.
4 Bats and foxes don't sleep **in** / **at** night.
5 My birthday is **in** / **at** the spring.
6 We play tennis **at** / **on** Fridays.
7 I always do my homework **in** / **on** the morning.
8 There's a music festival **in** / **on** 2nd May.

*2 Write the words in the correct place.

~~four o'clock~~   October   the evening   Mondays
the weekend   19th January   night   the winter
Friday morning   half past six   2006
his birthday   break-time

in	on	at
		four o'clock

*3 ▶ 22.1 Complete the conversations with *in*, *on* or *at*. Then listen and check. Use the questions to interview a partner.

▶ When did you start school?
   <u>In</u> 2006.

1 When do you do sport?
   _____ Mondays, Thursdays and Fridays.

2 Is your birthday _____ the autumn?
   No, it's _____ the spring.

3 When does this lesson finish?
   _____ quarter to three.

4 When do you brush your teeth?
   _____ the morning and _____ bedtime.

5 When will you next see your grandparents and cousins?
   _____ my birthday.

6 What do you have for breakfast _____ school days?
   Cereal and milk.

Time expressions

We also use the words **before**, **after**, **ago**, **every**, **this**, **last** and **next** to talk about time.

Before / after + noun / date / time
I did my homework **before** breakfast.
She bought it the day **before** yesterday.
We can go to a café **after** school.
I'll see you the day **after** tomorrow.

Time period + ago
I saw him five minutes **ago**.
Dinosaurs lived 200 million years **ago**.

Every + day / week / month / season / year
I play football **every** Saturday. (= on Saturdays)
We have a barbecue **every** summer.
I go to the dentist **every** six months.

This + part of day / week / month / year
I told you **this** morning! (= earlier today)
I'll tell you **this** afternoon. (= later today)
You must do your homework **this** week.

Last / next + day / week / month / year
The police came **last** Wednesday.
What are you doing **next** month?

I'll tidy my room before the weekend, OK?

You said that three weeks ago!

We use **last** and **next** in questions like this:
When did you **last** … ?
(= What was the last time that you … ?)
When will you **next** … ?
(= When will be the next time that you … ?)

— When did you **last** see Gemma?
— This morning.
— And when will you **next** see her?
— This evening.

4 Complete the sentences with the words in the box.

> ago ago after before every
> every ~~last~~ last next next

▶ I stayed there _last_ summer.
1 When will you _____ have a break?
2 I saw Fred the day _____ yesterday.
3 It happened six months _____ .
4 When did you _____ go on holiday?
5 Charlie's coming the day _____ tomorrow.
6 I go to Bella's house _____ Friday.
7 We're preparing for exams _____ month.
8 It all happened a long time _____ .
9 We have the same problem _____ winter.

5 ⏵ 22.2 Look at the calendar. Today is Wednesday 16th May. Write time expressions with *before, after, ago, every, this, last* and *next*. Then listen, check and repeat.

MAY								JUNE						
M	T	W	T	F	S	S		M	T	W	T	F	S	S
	1	2	3	4	5	6						1	2	3
7	8	9	10	11	12	13		4	5	6	7	8	9	10
14	15	(16)	17	18	19	20		11	12	13	14	15	16	17
21	22	23	24	25	26	27		18	19	20	21	22	23	24
28	29	30	31					25	26	27	28	29	30	

▶ Sunday 13th May = t_hree_ d_ays_ a_go_
1 June = n_____ m_____
2 2nd May = t_____ w_____ a_____
3 Friday 18th May = the d_____ a_____ t_____
4 23rd May, 30th May, 6th June, 13th June, 20th June = e_____ W_____
5 Monday 14th May = the d_____ b_____ _____y
6 7th–11th May = l_____ w_____
7 14th–18th May = t_____ w_____

Unit 22   **121**

6 ◉ 22.3 Quiz. Work in teams. Can you guess the answers? Then listen and check.

General knowledge quiz

▶ How often does the football World Cup take place?
A ☐ every two years
B ☑ every four years

1 When did France win the World Cup?
A ☐ in 1998
B ☐ in 2002

2 When were the first Ancient Olympic Games?
A ☐ about 1300 years ago
B ☐ about 2800 years ago

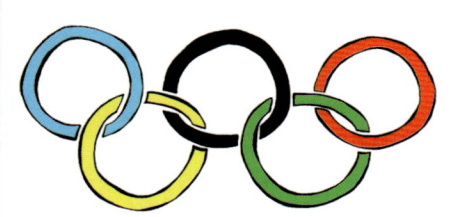

3 When did the first modern international Olympics take place?
A ☐ in 1896
B ☐ in 1924

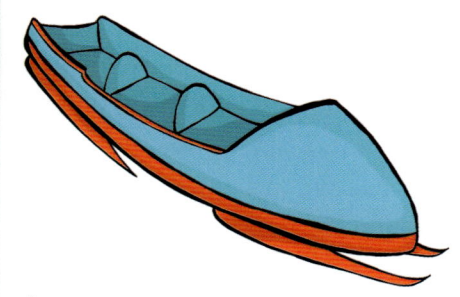

4 How often do the winter Olympics take place?
A ☐ every two years
B ☐ every four years

5 When do bears go to sleep for the winter?
A ☐ in October
B ☐ in December

6 And when do they wake up again?
A ☐ in February or March
B ☐ in April or May

7 When did the Internet begin?
A ☐ this century (2000–now)
B ☐ in the last century (1900–1999)

8 When did the Chinese invent fireworks?
A ☐ about 1400 years ago
B ☐ about 400 years ago

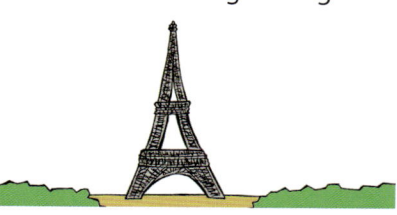

9 When did the French build the Eiffel Tower?
A ☐ after 1900
B ☐ before 1900

10 How often do people vote for President in the USA?
A ☐ every five years in December
B ☐ every four years in November

7 Delete the wrong phrase in each box.

▶ on my birthday
~~in 13th June~~
in the summer

1 every two or three hours
two or three hours ago
at two or three hours

2 on breakfast
at breakfast
after breakfast

3 at month
this month
last month

4 in 2010
in midnight
in February

5 45 minutes ago
a week ago
Monday ago

6 at July
in July
last July

7 on the last day of June
at the end of the day
in 31st January

8 this week
next 10 o'clock
last month

9 every Friday afternoon
on Friday afternoons
in Fridays

10 20th August ago
before 20th August
on 20th August

11 after evening
after the lesson
after ten o'clock

Prepositions of time

8 **GAME** Work in small groups. Take turns to answer a question. Move one square each time you get a question right. The first person to reach the finish is the winner.

When did you last eat some rice? Did you have some yesterday?

No, that's wrong. I had some two weeks ago.

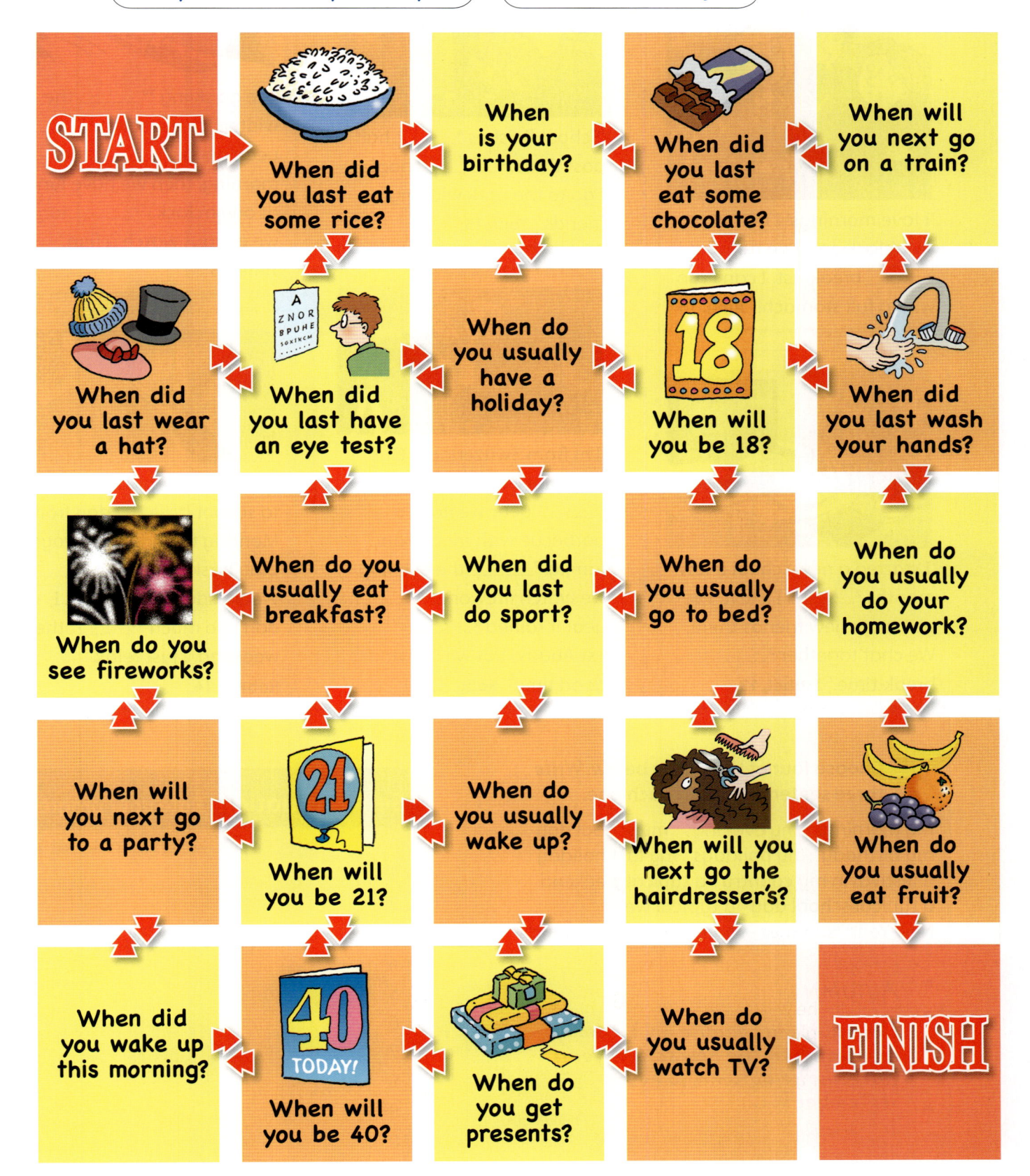

START

When did you last eat some rice?

When is your birthday?

When did you last eat some chocolate?

When will you next go on a train?

When did you last wear a hat?

When did you last have an eye test?

When do you usually have a holiday?

When will you be 18?

When did you last wash your hands?

When do you see fireworks?

When do you usually eat breakfast?

When did you last do sport?

When do you usually go to bed?

When do you usually do your homework?

When will you next go to a party?

When will you be 21?

When do you usually wake up?

When will you next go the hairdresser's?

When do you usually eat fruit?

When did you wake up this morning?

When will you be 40?

When do you get presents?

When do you usually watch TV?

FINISH

Unit 22 123

9 Add the missing prepositions and time expressions.

'I love mornings! I get up _at_ six o'clock and I go running ¹_____ breakfast. I can't run with a full stomach!' **Amy, 16**

'I started a new school a few months ²_____. I like it. I've got some new friends there. We chat together ³_____ break-time.' **Isabel, 13**

'School finishes ⁴_____ half past three. ⁵_____ school, I go to the park with my friends.' **Tom, 13**

'I'm from Switzerland. Our National Day is 1st August. ⁶_____ year we have a barbecue with friends and family. ⁷_____ the evening we watch fireworks. ⁸_____ year it rained ⁹_____ 1st August but we still had a good time.' **Sally, 15**

'We go skiing ¹⁰_____ the winter. It's the same ¹¹_____ year: we ski ¹²_____ the morning, then we have lunch at one o'clock. ¹³_____ lunch we always watch a film.' **Jane, 13**

'What's my typical week? I go to school ¹⁴_____ day from Monday to Friday. I always play basketball ¹⁵_____ Wednesday afternoons. I don't do much ¹⁶_____ the weekend. I just relax.' **Robert, 14**

10 Choose four of the topics below. Write three sentences about each one.

my mornings   my evenings   my school day
my birthday   my holidays   my last holiday
a festival in my country   a typical weekend
a typical school day   a typical week
New Year   summer   winter   autumn   spring

AUTUMN

I like autumn because my birthday is in October. The new school year starts in the autumn, so every September I …

Self-evaluation Rate your progress.

	😊	😊😊	😊😊😊
1			
2			
3			
4			
5			
6			
7			
8			
9			
10			

Prepositions of time

Revision 6 — Units 21–22

Reading and writing

1 Look and read. Write 'yes' or 'no'.

▶ There is a cup on the table. _yes_
1 The woman is sitting next to the window. ____
2 There is a red suitcase above the man. ____
3 There is a green rucksack under the woman's seat. ____
4 There is a newspaper between the man and the woman. ____
5 The train is at a station. ____

2 Read the email. Choose the correct words from the box and write them next to 1–7.

| ago | after | ~~at~~ | before | between | every |
| in | in | last | near | next | on | this |

Dear Jason,

Would you like to come and stay with me and my family _at_ the weekend? We're going to be ¹_____ our holiday cottage ²_____ the sea. We go there ³_____ year. It's in a beautiful location, ⁴_____ a lake and a forest. We will spend some time ⁵_____ the beach and maybe have a barbecue ⁶_____ the evening. What do you think? Let me know.

Frank

P.S. I phoned you ⁷_____ night but there was no answer. Where were you?

3 Read the email. Choose the right words and write them on the lines.

Inti Raymi (or 'Festival of the Sun') is an important Andean celebration. It takes place _every_ summer ¹_____ Cusco, Peru. The festival started during the Inca Empire, about 800 years ²_____.

Every year ³_____ June, many visitors go to Sacsayhuamán, an area ⁴_____ Cuzco, to see a theatrical performance of Inti Raymi. This tradition started ⁵_____ 1944.

▶ at (every) on   3 in on at
1 on this in   4 near against on
2 last ago before   5 in on at

4 Read the letter and write the missing words. Write one word on each line.

Dear Mr Carr,   2 July

Thank you for your application. We would like to invite you for an interview _on_ Wednesday 18 July ¹_____ 10.30 a.m. Please come to our central office. It is located ²_____ the first floor of Cavendish House, 29 Milton Road. You are welcome to stay for lunch ³_____ the interview. This will be served for all interview candidates ⁴_____ the Garden Room. Please let us know ⁵_____ week (before 6 July) if you would like to attend the interview.

Yours sincerely
Mary White

Listening

5 ▶ R12.1 Listen and write.

HILLVIEW SUMMER CAMP TIMETABLE
▶ Tennis lessons: Where? In the sports hall
(_next to_ the swimming pool)
1 Tennis lessons: When? At ten o'clock _____
2 Music session: When? _____
3 Music session: Where? In the room _____ the café
4 Film: When? _____, at four o'clock.
5 Film: Where? In Room 4, _____ Reception

6 ▶ R12.2 Listen and tick ✓ the correct picture.

▶ Where is Debbie?

1 Where are the theatre tickets?

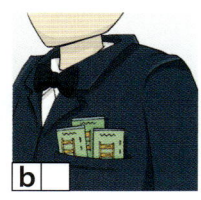

2 Where is the theatre?

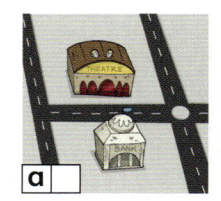

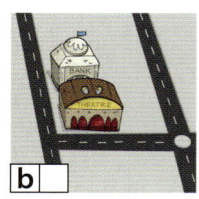

3 When did Andy last go to the theatre?

Speaking

7 Work in pairs. Look at the pictures. Can you find 10 differences?

Picture 1

Picture 2

In picture 1 the handbag is on the chair but in picture 2 it's on the floor near the door.

126 Units 21–22

23 Question words

I can recognize and use question words.

Who, where, what, when, why, how

We use question words (**who**, **where**, **what**, **when**, **why** and **how**) when we ask for information.
Questions with question words usually have the same word order as **yes/no** questions.

Do you like it? Yes, I like it.
Why do you like it?

Is he leaving? Yes, he's leaving.
When is he leaving?

Did it happen? Yes, it happened.
How did it happen?

Will you go? Yes, I'll go.
Where will you go?

Did you do it? Yes, I did it.
What did you do?

We often use **who** as the subject of a question, without **do**, **does** or **did**.

Who likes pizza?
Who wrote this?

We can also use it in the same pattern as a **yes/no** question.

Can you talk to someone?
Yes, I can talk to someone.
Who can you talk to?

Speech bubbles:
What's in that box?
I don't know.
Where has it come from?
Italy.
Who sent it?
My grandparents.
How do you know?
Because of the stamps and the writing.
When are you going to open it?
Now! But please stop asking questions!

*1 **Circle the correct question word.**

▶ Why / (When) does the film start?
　At seven o'clock.

1　Who / Where has the books?
　Kate.

2　What / How will you open it?
　With the key.

3　Where / What did you eat?
　At home.

4　What / Where did you eat?
　Chicken and rice.

5　Where / Why is he at the hospital?
　He's visiting George.

6　Who / How did you talk to?
　Lots of people.

7　Who / What said that?
　Me.

8　How / When are you meeting him?
　Tomorrow.

9　Who / Where is your best friend?
　John Davies.

10　What / Who are you going to do?
　I'll phone the police.

2 Complete the questions with the words below.

> how   how   what   when   where
> where   ~~who~~   who   who   why   why

▶ 💬 _Who_ are you going with?
  💬 My sister.

1 💬 _____ are you sad?
  💬 Because I failed my exam.

2 💬 _____ did you go?
  💬 To the shops.

3 💬 _____ is your teacher?
  💬 Mrs Harris.

4 💬 _____ did you break it?
  💬 I dropped it.

5 💬 _____ is Perth?
  💬 In Australia.

6 💬 _____ said that?
  💬 Anna.

7 💬 _____ did he buy?
  💬 A notebook.

8 💬 _____ can we meet?
  💬 How about Friday?

9 💬 _____ do you get to school?
  💬 I walk.

10 💬 _____ did you say that?
   💬 Because it's true!

3 ▶ 23.1 Listen and answer the question about pronunciation. Then listen again and repeat. Do the last words in these questions go up ↗ or down ↘?

Who makes you laugh?
Who do you live with?

4 Read these sentences. Be sure to make your voice go up and down correctly.

Who makes you laugh?
Who makes you cry?
Who do you live with?
Who do you talk with?
Who do you learn with?

5 Write down your answers to the questions in exercise 4. Then ask and answer the questions with a partner.

> Who makes you laugh?   My brother.

6 **GAME** Work in pairs. Read the sentences and think about your partner. Circle the answer you think is true or write your own answer. Ask your partner questions. How many of your guesses were right?

I think my partner …

- drank tea / coffee / milk / juice / hot chocolate at breakfast.
- came to school by bus / by car / on foot / by train today.
- is planning to study / do sports / watch TV / meet friends at the weekend.
- last bought something this morning / yesterday / two days ago / a week ago / a long time ago.
- will go on holiday with friends / family / friends and family next year.
- is going home / to a club / to a friend's house / to the park after school today.

> how   what   what   when   where   who

> What did you drink at breakfast?   Juice.
> I was right! And how did you come to school today?   On foot.
> Oh. I was wrong!

Question words

Questions with **what** + noun and **how** + adjective / adverb

We can ask questions with **what** + noun.
What kind of music do you like?
What time is it?
What colour are her eyes?

We also ask questions with **how** + adjective / adverb.
How long is the film?
How high is that mountain?

We ask questions about quantity with **how many** and **how much**. (For more information, see unit 3.)
How many sisters have you got?
How much water have we got?

*7 ▶ 23.2 **Complete the conversation with *what* or *how*. Listen and check. Then act out the conversation with a partner.**

💬 What did you do yesterday?
💭 I went fishing at the lake.
💬 _How_ long did you stay there?
💭 About forty-five minutes.
💬 ¹_____ many fish did you catch?
💭 Just one.
💬 ²_____ big was it?
💭 About 50 or 60 cm – like this.
💬 ³_____ kind of fish was it?
💭 I'm not sure.
💬 ⁴_____ colour was it?
💭 Grey.
💬 ⁵_____ heavy was it?
💭 About one kilo.
💬 ⁶_____ did you do with it?
💭 I put it back in the water.

*8 **Work in pairs. Act out the fishing conversation again. Change the answers to questions 1-6 to make your own story.**

How long did you stay there?

About two hours.

*9 **Complete the questions with the words below.**

~~big~~   fast   kind   many   much   often   size   time   well

▶ 💬 How _big_ was it?
💭 The same size as a cat.

1 💬 How _____ do you wash your hair?
💭 Every day.

2 💬 What _____ did you get home?
💭 About ten o'clock.

3 💬 How _____ does he play tennis?
💭 He's an excellent player.

4 💬 How _____ did that game cost?
💭 £40.

5 💬 What _____ do you want?
💭 Medium, please.

6 💬 What _____ of bird was it?
💭 A parrot.

7 💬 How _____ exams are there?
💭 Five.

8 💬 How _____ can you drive on the motorway?
💭 70 miles per hour.

Unit 23   **129**

10 Write the questions in the correct order. Then use the questions to interview a partner.

▶ this / how / lesson / is / long
<u>How long is this lesson?</u>

1 got / cousins / how / you / many / have
_____

2 did / who / you / breakfast with / have
_____

3 sort of / what / do / like / you / music
_____

4 today / water / drunk / have / much / you / how
_____

5 where / you / your homework / do / do
_____

6 are / you / why / wearing / shoes / those
_____

7 walls / are / your / colour / bedroom / what
_____

8 by / how / you / often / do / travel / bus
_____

9 wake up / what / you / time / did
_____

10 you / did / last / a photo / when / take
_____

11 Complete the second question so that it means the same as the first. Use three, four or five words. Then interview a partner.

▶ Do you live in the city centre, near the city or in a village?
<u>Where do you</u> live?

1 Did you get up at six o'clock or seven o'clock today?
What _____ get up today?

2 Can you ride a bike very well or not very well?
_____ ride a bike?

3 Have you got blue eyes, green eyes or brown eyes?
What _____ got?

4 Are you learning English because you want to or because you have to?
_____ learning English?

12 GAME How many questions? Work in teams. Think of as many questions for each statement as you can. The team with the most questions wins.

I've got a new bike.

I can speak French and Japanese.

I'm going to see a film tonight.

My aunt's just had a baby.

I've got an appointment with the dentist today.

I've got some new shoes.

130 Question words

13 GAME
General knowledge quiz. Work in two teams, A and B. Team A look at the information on this page. Team B look at the information on page 155.

Team A
1 Prepare quiz questions from the information.
2 Ask team B your quiz questions.
3 Answer questions from team B.
4 The team with the most correct answers wins.

How old is Machu Pichu?

I think it's 400 years old.

No, it's 600 years old!

Machu Picchu
Machu Picchu is around 600 years old. It is 2,400 metres above sea level.

1 200 / 400 / 600 years old?
   How old is Machu Picchu?
2 2400 / 2600 / 2500 metres above sea level?

Crocodile, baby crocodile
A crocodile has about 65 teeth. A baby crocodile is only about 20cm long.

3 65 / 75 / 85 teeth?

4 baby crocodile: 20cm / 50cm / 80cm long?

The human brain
The human brain uses about 25 per cent of the glucose in our blood for energy. It is not fully developed until we are 18 years old.

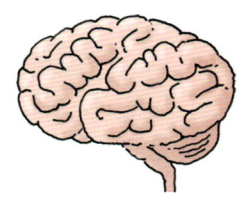

5 brain fully developed: 14 / 18 / 25 years old?

6 brain uses 15% / 25% / 40% glucose in our blood for energy?

14
Imagine you can interview your favourite film star, pop star or sportsperson. Write fifteen questions for the interview. Use question words. Ask about the topics below.

The past
childhood memories   school days
important experiences

Now
daily routine   likes and dislikes
special places   important people

The future
hopes   goals   dreams   plans

QUESTIONS FOR … (name)
1 Where were you born?
2 What did you like at school?

Self-evaluation Rate your progress.

	🙂	🙂🙂	🙂🙂🙂
1			
2			
3			
4			
5			
6			
7			
8			
9			
10			
11			
12			
13			
14			

24 Question tags

I can recognize and use question tags in conversation and to check information.

This is the right house, isn't it?
Yes, I think so.

A question tag is a short question that we can add at the end of a statement. We form it with the auxiliary verb + subject.

The subject of the tag and the statement are the same. The auxiliary verb in the tag reflects the verb in the statement.

You're coming with us, **aren't you**?
The film has already started, **hasn't it**?
Gabriel speaks Russian, **doesn't he**?
They stayed a long time, **didn't they**?

A positive statement has a negative tag.

+	−
I can leave it here,	can't I?
You'll like that,	won't you?
She understands,	doesn't she?
He told you the story,	didn't he?
I'm right,	aren't I?

Note: *I'm right, aren't I?* (~~amn't I?~~)

A negative statement has a positive tag.

−	+
You weren't angry,	were you?
She couldn't do it,	could she?
It isn't very nice,	is it?
You've never met Lee,	have you?

*1 ▶ 24.1 What are the people in the picture saying? Match 1–6 with a–f. Then listen and check.

a 3
b
c
d
e
f

1 He looks happy, doesn't he?
2 That was a big meal, wasn't it?
3 ~~It's cold today, isn't it?~~
4 She's going to win, isn't she?
5 He can't get it, can he?
6 We haven't met before, have we?

*2 ▶ 24.2 Choose the correct tag. Then listen, check your answers and repeat the sentences.

▶ She wasn't here,
   ☑ was she?   ☐ wasn't she?

1 It isn't easy,
   ☐ is it?   ☐ isn't it?
2 Alice can't swim,
   ☐ can she?   ☐ can't she?
3 You like this music,
   ☐ do you?   ☐ don't you?
4 He saw us,
   ☐ did he?   ☐ didn't he?
5 You've lost your ticket,
   ☐ have you?   ☐ haven't you?
6 You aren't going to do it,
   ☐ are you?   ☐ aren't you?
7 I'm fast,
   ☐ am I?   ☐ aren't I?
8 This has never happened before,
   ☐ has it?   ☐ hasn't it?

3 ▶ 24.3 Circle the correct answer. Then listen, check your answers and repeat the sentences.

▶ She **'s** / **was** swimming, wasn't she?
1 Philip **hasn't phoned** / **didn't phone**, has he?
2 Jane **plays** / **played** tennis, didn't she?
3 It **'s going to** / **will** work, won't it?
4 They **can't** / **couldn't** do it, could they?
5 You **'re eating** / **eat** fish, don't you?
6 He **isn't going to leave** / **hasn't left**, is he?
7 This programme **'s** / **was** interesting, isn't it?
8 You **'re not leaving** / **won't leave**, are you?

4 Add the correct subject from the box to each tag.

they they it ~~you~~ he we you she I

▶ You're Italian, aren't _you_ ?
1 They were happy, weren't _____?
2 I can wear this hat, can't _____?
3 Your sister's passed her exam, hasn't _____?
4 Kate and Charlie didn't know, did _____?
5 The music was good, wasn't _____?
6 You and your sister play golf, don't _____?
7 Your dad's a pilot, isn't _____?
8 You and I have the same surname, don't _____?

5 GAME Work in three teams, A, B and C. Read the instructions and play the game.

Instructions
Take turns to make sentences with the question tags below.
When you use a tag correctly, you 'win' it and write your team's letter on it (A, B or C).
When you 'win' a tag it is out of action for the rest of the game.
Think fast! You only have 10 seconds for your turn!
The team with the most tags at the end wins the game.

_____ ✂ _____ ?

- hasn't she?
- can't she?
- aren't we?
- haven't you?
- isn't it?
- will we?
- weren't you?
- has he?
- am I?
- doesn't it?
- didn't they?
- Have I?
- didn't they?
- aren't I?
- shouldn't we?
- won't we?
- wasn't he?
- don't you?
- can he?
- did he?

It's your turn, team B.

OK ... the 'don't you?' tag. You walk to school, don't you?

Correct sentence. You win the tag.

- ~~don't you?~~ B

Unit 24 133

Question tags in conversation

It was a funny film, wasn't it?
Yes, it was. I laughed a lot!

We can use question tags to make conversation.
It's a lovely day, **isn't it?**
Lucas didn't like it, **did he?**
Here, the tag means: 'I think you will agree with my statement.'

6 Add the correct tags to the conversations.

have you? is it? did she? can she? won't it?
hasn't he? were they? don't you? doesn't he?

▶ You like cheese, <u>don't you?</u>
   No, I don't, actually.
1 He has lunch at school, _____
   Yes, he does.
2 She can't ski, _____
   Yes, she can, actually.
3 He's got a dog, _____
   Yes, I think so.
4 It isn't funny, _____
   No, it isn't.
5 It'll be cold, _____
   No, I don't think so.
6 You've never been to Italy, _____
   Yes, I have! Lots of times!
7 Jim and Alice weren't playing, _____
   No, they weren't.
8 She didn't phone, _____
   No.

7 Look again at exercise 6. Does speaker 2 agree or disagree with speaker 1 in each conversation? Write A (agree) or D (disagree).

▶ <u>D</u>   2 ___   4 ___   6 ___   8 ___
1 ___   3 ___   5 ___   7 ___

8 Complete the questions with question tags. Then add responses from the box below.

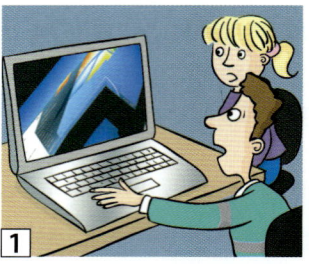

No, he might fall.
Actually, I fell asleep in the middle.
~~Yes, the view's amazing.~~
Actually, I think it's too big.
Yes, I don't understand.
No, I think it's got a virus.

▶ It's beautiful here, <u>isn't it?</u>
   <u>Yes, the view's amazing.</u>
1 It's not working, _____
   _____
2 He shouldn't do that, _____
   _____
3 It's strange, _____
   _____
4 The new TV's great, _____
   _____
5 That was exciting, _____
   _____

9 ▶ 24.4 Listen and check your answers to exercise 8. Then act out the conversations with a partner.

134 Question tags

Question tags to check information

We use question tags to check information.

*79 plus 21 makes 100, **doesn't it**?*
*You eat meat, **don't you**?*

Here, the tag means:
'Is the statement correct?'

Egypt's in Europe, isn't it?
Yes, I think so.
No, it isn't! Egypt is in Africa.

10 ▶ 24.5 Listen to people checking information. Where are the mistakes?

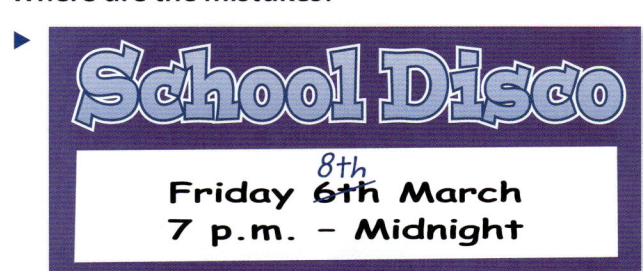

▶ **School Disco**
Friday ~~6th~~ 8th March
7 p.m. – Midnight

1. Charlie Jenkins phoned about Saturday job
   Age: 16

2.
   1. Paris
   2. red, white and blue
   3. about 65,000
   4. 14th July

3. Richard ✓ Mary ✗
   Jack ✓ Bella ✓

4. Largest rainforest in the world — Produces 20% of the world's oxygen — The Amazon Rainforest — Has 2m plant and animal species — Nine different countries — Most of it is in Ecuador

11 ▶ 24.6 Add the question tags. Listen and check, then practise reading the conversations with a partner.

▶ 💬 Your sister's left school now, <u>hasn't she?</u>
   💬 No, she finishes next summer.
   💬 Oh, OK.

1. 💬 You went to the USA last year, _____
   💬 Yeah, we had a really good time.

2. 💬 A spider's got six legs.
   💬 No, it's got eight legs, _____
   💬 Oh yes, I think you're right.

3. 💬 I will see you again, _____
   💬 Of course you will! Don't worry.

4. 💬 It's made of glass.
   💬 No, it's made of plastic, _____
   💬 No, it's definitely glass. Feel it.
   💬 Oh yes.

5. 💬 James can swim, _____
   💬 No, I don't think he can, actually.

6. 💬 It isn't raining, _____
   💬 Yes, I'm afraid it is.

Unit 24 **135**

12 What personal information would you like to check? Work in groups. Write sentences with tag questions for the people in your group. Use these topics.

birthdays   hobbies   family   likes and dislikes
experiences   habits and routines   future plans

- Paul, your birthday's in June, isn't it?
- Molly, you like rock music, don't you?
- Andy, you've got two brothers, haven't you?
- Sarah, you're going to swimming club tomorrow, aren't you?

13 Talk in groups. Use your sentences with question tags from exercise 12 to check if your ideas are correct.

Paul, your birthday's in June, isn't it?

No, it's in July. Molly, you like rock music, don't you?

Yes, that's right.

14 GAME Work in small groups. There are ten errors (scientific, historical, mathematical, geographical) in this picture. Can you spot them? Look at page 154 to find the answers.

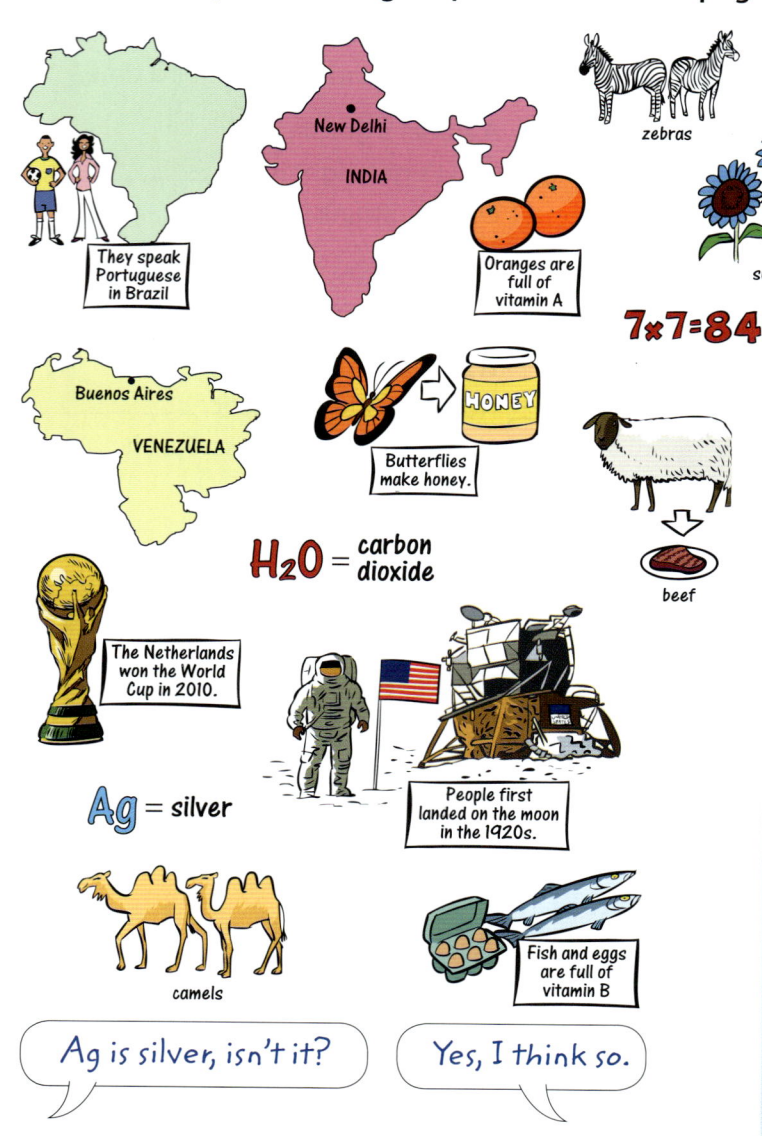

- They speak Portuguese in Brazil
- New Delhi, INDIA
- Oranges are full of vitamin A
- zebras
- sunflowers
- $7 \times 7 = 84$
- Leonardo da Vinci painted the Mona Lisa.
- Elephants can't jump.
- $11 \times 11 = 121$
- Vesuvius is in Italy
- Buenos Aires, VENEZUELA
- Butterflies make honey.
- H_2O = carbon dioxide
- beef
- The Netherlands won the World Cup in 2010.
- People first landed on the moon in the 1920s.
- Ag = silver
- camels
- Fish and eggs are full of vitamin B

Ag is silver, isn't it? *Yes, I think so.*

Self-evaluation Rate your progress.

	🙂	🙂🙂	🙂🙂🙂
1			
2			
3			
4			
5			
6			
7			
8			
9			
10			
11			
12			
13			
14			

Revision 7 — Units 23–24

Reading and writing

1 Match 1–5 with a–h to complete the conversation. You don't have to use all the letters.

▶ 💬 b
  💬 I'm fine, thanks.

1 💬 ___
  💬 Yes, I went to the cinema.

2 💬 ___
  💬 Joe and Heidi.

3 💬 ___
  💬 'Down in the City'.

4 💬 ___
  💬 Yes, it is.

5 💬 ___
  💬 About half past ten.

a That's a really long film, isn't it?
b How are you?
c What kind of film is that?
d You went out last night, didn't you?
e Who did you go with?
f What time did you get home?
g What film did you see?
h How long did it last?

2 Read the emails. Choose a word from the box. Write the correct word next to numbers 1–5.

| how | is | many | much | kind | what | when | where | who | why |

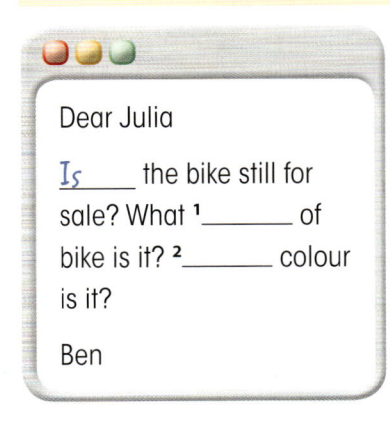

Dear Julia

Is___ the bike still for sale? What ¹_____ of bike is it? ² _____ colour is it?

Ben

FOR SALE
Bicycle: £30
Contact Julia at Julia_21@onmail.com

TO RENT
Holiday Cottage for six people; beautiful views
£450 a week
Email Tom at tom854@vmail.com

Dear Tom

I'm interested in your holiday cottage, but I'd like some more information. ³_____ is it? How ⁴_____ bedrooms does it have? ⁵_____ big is the garden? Can you send me a photo?

Thanks
Bella Lyell

3 Read the letters and write the missing words. Write one word on each line.

Dear Oscar

Where are you? ¹_____ haven't you answered my phone calls? I'm worried about you. You remember Julia, ²_____ you? She gave me your address. I asked, '³_____ did you last speak to Oscar?' and she replied, 'I don't know. It was a long time ago.' Now she's worried about you too. You are OK, ⁴_____ you?

Please, please write.
Ivy

Dear Ivy

Thank you for your letter. You sent your letter to my old address. I've moved house and started a new school. I didn't hear your phone calls. How ⁵_____ times did you call? When? You've got the Internet, ⁶_____ you? I've put my email address at the end of this letter. You will write again, ⁷_____ you? It was so good to hear from you.

Oscar

P.S. ⁸_____ is Julia?

Revision 7 137

Listening

4 ▶ R13.1 Listen and tick ✓ the correct picture.

▶ Where are Paul and Sandra?

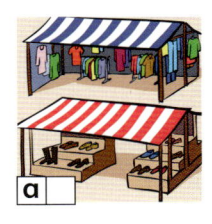

a ☐ b ✓ c ☐

1 Why does Paul need new shoes?

a ☐ b ☐ c ☐

2 How does Paul pay for the shoes?

a ☐ b ☐ c ☐

5 ▶ R13.2 Listen and draw lines.

Mike   Dave   Vicky

Sidney   Carla   Mandy

Speaking

6 Work in pairs. Student A look at the information below and student B turn to page 157. Complete the table. Ask your partner questions to get the information you need. Use the prompts.

Bus to city centre

bus stop / it leave from	number 9
long / the journey	forty-five minutes
much / a single ticket cost	three pounds
often / the bus leave	every ten minutes
time / next bus	2.20
where / buy a ticket?	on the bus

Train to city centre

platform / it leave from	
long / the journey	
much / a single ticket cost	
often / the train leave	
time / next train	
where / buy a ticket?	

What bus stop does the bus to the city centre leave from?

Number nine.

What platform does the train to the city centre leave from?

Number seven.

138 Units 23–24

25 Conjunctions

I can recognize and use the conjunctions **and**, **but**, **or**, **because** and **so** to link ideas in sentences.

And, but and or

We use conjunctions to link ideas together when we speak or write. We use them to show ideas like similarity, difference, reason, options, and result or consequence.

*I like it **but** it's very hot **and** spicy!*

*I like it **because** it's hot **and** spicy!*

We use **and** to link two similar ideas in one sentence.
The sun's shining. It's 31°C.
The sun's shining **and** it's 31°C.
It's sunny **and** warm.

We use **but** to contrast two different ideas in one sentence.
The sun's shining. It's -5°C.
The sun's shining **but** it's -5°C.
It's sunny **but** cold.

We use **or** to talk about two different possibilities or options.
We can sit outside. We can sit inside.
We can sit outside **or** inside.
Do you want to sit here **or** go inside?

*1 Choose the correct conjunction.
  ▶ She has black hair **and** / or brown eyes.
  1 Would you like to stay in **and** / **or** go out this evening?
  2 I have a bike **or** / **but** I don't use it.
  3 I can play the guitar **and** / **but** the piano.
  4 I think she's a doctor **but** / **or** a teacher. I'm not sure.
  5 I like pizza **and** / **but** I don't like pasta.
  6 That tiger is beautiful **but** / **or** it's very dangerous.

*2 Read and complete the sentences with *and*, *but* or *or*.
  ▶ All my friends liked the film …
    … _but_ I thought it was boring.
    … _and_ I loved it too.
  1 You can have chocolate sauce …
    … _____ you have to pay extra.
    … _____ strawberry sauce.
  2 I was late for school …
    … _____ I missed the first lesson.
    … _____ I didn't miss the exam.
  3 Would you like to go to the beach …
    … _____ go to the mountains?
    … _____ have a swim in the sea?

Unit 25 139

3 Match 1–7 with a–h and add *and*, *but* or *or*.

▶ I could come at 1 _b_
1 Do you want a pen ___
2 He's very kind ___
3 She likes walking ___
4 Was it easy ___
5 It was difficult ___
6 There were lots of sheep ___
7 We can stop now ___

a _____ running.
b _or_ 2 o'clock.
c _____ have a break.
d _____ no cows.
e _____ helpful.
f _____ a pencil?
g _____ I did it.
h _____ difficult?

4 GAME Play this memory game in small groups. Take turns to add an item to the list.

I went to the shop and I bought a pen.

I went to the shop and I bought a pen and an apple.

I went to the shop and I bought a pen, an apple and a hat.

I went to the shop and …

5 Talk in pairs. How many ways can you finish these sentences?

Computers are expensive but …
Snow is beautiful but …
Money is important but …
Chocolate is nice but …
Cars are useful but …
Sunshine gives us vitamin D but …

Computers are expensive but they are useful.

6 ▶ 25.1 Listen. Which intonation pattern do all the questions below have – a, b or c? Listen again and repeat the sentences.

a
b
c

1 Do you prefer hot food or cold food? ___
2 Are you over the age of 12 or under the age of 12? ___
3 Do you prefer watching sports or doing sports? ___
4 Do you live in a house or a flat? ___

7 Use the questions in exercise 6 to interview a partner.

8 Work with a partner. Take turns to ask questions about the choices. Use *Do you … or … ?* or *Are you … or … ?* and the prompts.

Do you prefer chess or computer games?

I prefer computer games because they're more exciting, but I like chess too.

▶  chess / computer games
1  books / TV
2  only child / brothers and sisters
3  cats / dogs
4 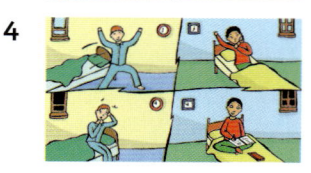 a morning person / an evening person

140 Conjunctions

Because and so

Because and so are conjuctions. We use because to give the reason for a fact or situation. It answers questions with Why?

Fact or situation	Reason
He's got wet hair.	He's been swimming.
He's got wet hair **because** he's been swimming.	

It's cold **because** the window's open.
I'm happy **because** I passed my exams.

In writing we usually use **because** in the middle of a sentence. In speech we can also use it at the beginning of a sentence.

💬 Why has he got wet hair?
💬 **Because** he's been swimming in the sea.

We use **so** to talk about the result of something. It answers the question What happens next?

Fact or situation	Result
She felt ill.	She went to the doctor.
She felt ill **so** she went to the doctor.	

I was tired **so** I went to bed.
The birds were beautiful **so** I took a lot of photos.

*9 ▶ 25.2 Listen and tick ✓ the correct picture.
  ▶ Why didn't you come to the party?   
     a ✓   b ☐   c ☐
  1 Why aren't there any more biscuits?   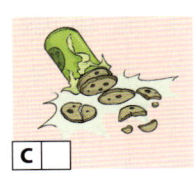
     a ☐   b ☐   c ☐
  2 Why are you late for school?   
     a ☐   b ☐   c ☐
  3 Why are you going to the supermarket?   
     a ☐   b ☐   c ☐
  4 Why have you got that backpack?
     a ☐   b ☐   c ☐

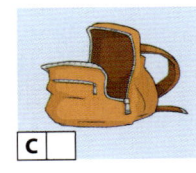

*10 Work in pairs. Ask and answer questions from exercise 9. Think of different reasons.

  Why didn't you come to the party?
  Because I was on holiday.

*11 Choose the correct conjunction.
  ▶ I live a long way from school **because** /(**so**) I go by bus.
  1 He's hungry **because** / **so** he didn't have any breakfast this morning.
  2 You broke it **because** / **so** you can pay for a new one!
  3 Fish makes Alison ill **because** / **so** she never eats it.
  4 The Atacama Desert is dry **because** / **so** it hardly ever rains there.
  5 Ryan wanted to buy a new computer **because** / **so** he got a job.
  6 I woke up early **because** / **so** I went for a walk.
  7 She can't walk **because** / **so** she's hurt her leg.

12 ▶ **25.3** Listen to two people playing a game. Tick all the 'odd ones out' they find.

Odd one out

Rules of the game
Work in small teams. Find as many 'odd ones out' as you can.

Group 1

| zebra | tiger | fish ✓ | whale ✓ |

Group 2

| cup | glass | mug | vase |

Group 3

| doctor | taxi driver | teacher | thief |

Points
2 points for every 'odd one out' you find.
5 points for an 'odd one out' reason that no other team thinks of.

---

13 ▶ **25.4** Circle the correct conjunctions in the conversation. Then listen again and check.

💬 Group 1 – the zebra, the tiger and the fish all have two colours **or** / **(but)** the whale is only one colour, ¹ **so** / **because** the whale is the 'odd one out'.

💬 Yes, ² **but** / **because** the fish is also the 'odd one out'.

💬 Why?

💬 ³ **And** / **Because** the others are all animals.

💬 ⁴ **Or** / **But** the whale is a fish!

💬 No, it isn't. It lives in the water but it isn't a fish ⁵ **or** / **because** it has to have air.

💬 Oh, yes!

14 ▶ **25.5** Complete the second part of the conversation with the conjunctions in the box. Then listen again and check.

but   or   ~~because~~   so   and   because

💬 Group 2 – well, the vase is the 'odd one out' <u>because</u> it isn't for drinks ¹_____ the cup is the 'odd one out' because it hasn't got flowers on it.

💬 OK. Group 3. The doctor's the only woman ²_____ she's the 'odd one out'.

💬 Yes, and the thief's the 'odd one out' because the teacher, the taxi driver and the doctor all help people ³_____ the thief doesn't help people.

💬 And the teacher is the 'odd one out' ⁴_____ she works in the day but the others all – sometimes ⁵_____ always – work at night.

💬 Brilliant!

15 **GAME** Work in pairs. Find the 'odd ones out' in each group. Use the points system from exercise 12.

Group 4

| sandals | flip flops | T-shirt | boots |

Group 5

| roller blades | speedboats | cars | bicycles |

Group 6

| mouse | jellyfish | bee | scorpion |

💬 *The sandals are the 'odd one out' because they aren't blue.*

💬 *And the T-shirt is the 'odd one out' because ...*

142 Conjunctions

16 Work in pairs. Read the letter from a magazine and make decisions about your trip. Think about the reasons for your decisions. Make notes.

Around the world in six weeks!

Congratulations! You have won a 'round-the-world' travel ticket! You and a friend and your two families can travel around the world for six weeks – free!

Now it's time to make some important decisions!

1 Route
Which way around the world would you like to travel?

Option A: east to west

Option B: west to east

Shall we ... or ...?

2 Cities
Which cities would you like to stop in? Choose SIX.
If you're not sure where they are, find them on a map.

Toronto   St Petersburg
   Moscow   Seoul
New York   Oxford   Tokyo
London   Paris
   Bangkok
   Cairo
Los Angeles   Shanghai
   Mumbai
Mexico City   Cape Town
Rio de Janeiro   Canberra

*I'd like to go to ... and ...
I like ... so ...
Would you prefer to go to ... or ...?*

3 Transport
How would you like to travel?

by coach    by ship    on horseback

by hot-air balloon

*I'd like to do this part of the journey by ... because ...
It's a long way from ... to ... so I think we should ...*

4 Luggage
What form of luggage will you take? Choose ONE.

backpack    suitcases

... is better because ...

5 Equipment
What will you take? Choose FIVE.

*We need to take ... because ...
We don't need to take ... because ...
It will be cold in ... so ...*

17 Tell the rest of the class about your plans in exercise 16.

We're going to travel from west to east because ...

18 Write to the magazine about your plans for your trip around the world.

*Thank you for my prize!
We'd like to travel from west to east because ...*

Unit 25   143

19 Choose the correct answer.

▶ Has she got blue eyes or ___ eyes?
  a green ✓   b she got green ☐

1 I don't like it because ___.
  a boring ☐   b it's boring ☐

2 She can sing and ___.
  a can dance ☐   b dance ☐

3 You can have a sandwich or ___ hot food.
  a some ☐   b can have some ☐

4 It's nice but ___ very expensive.
  a it's ☐   b is ☐

5 It started raining so ___ home.
  a we went ☐   b went ☐

6 Do you prefer maths or ___?
  a art ☐   b prefer art ☐

20 Choose three of the topics below. Write a short paragraph about each one. Use *and*, *or*, *but*, *because* or *so* to link ideas in your sentences.

A long journey
Where did you go?   Why was it a long journey?
How did you feel?

A time I was ill
Why did you get ill?   How did you feel?
What happened?

A time I was late for something
What were you late for?   Why were you late?
What happened?

When I received a gift
Who gave you the gift?   Why did they give it
How did you feel?   to you?

When I gave a gift
Who did you give it to?   Why did you give it
How did they feel?   to them?

A LONG JOURNEY
I went to the beach in the car with my family. It was a long journey because there was a lot of traffic on the roads and ...

21 Join the pairs of sentences to make one sentence. Use *and*, *or*, *but*, *because* and *so*. The new sentence will be the number of words in brackets.

▶ It's beautiful. It's very expensive. (6 words)
  It's beautiful but it's very expensive.

1 I want to go home. I'm cold. (8 words)
  _____

2 You can do it now. You can do it later. (7 words)
  _____

3 I didn't feel well. I went home early. (9 words)
  _____

4 He can ski. He can snowboard. (5 words)
  _____

5 I started the book. I didn't finish it. (9 words)
  _____

6 I've studied conjunctions. Now I can use them correctly. (10 words)
  _____

Self-evaluation Rate your progress.

	😊	😊😊	😊😊😊
1			
2			
3			
4			
5			
6			
7			
8			
9			
10			
11			
12			
13			
14			
15			
16			
17			
18			
19			
20			
21			

26 Zero conditional

I can recognize and use the zero conditional.

If a chameleon wants to hide on yellow sand, its skin goes yellow.

Yes, and the skin changes colour if the chameleon is angry, too.

We use zero conditional sentences to describe things that always happen.

We also use it to talk about things that happen in the same way every time. These can be scientific or technical facts, or personal habits.
If you mix red and yellow **you get** orange.
He doesn't go out if the weather's bad.

Conditional sentences show a link between two events.

All conditional sentences are formed of two clauses. The 'condition' clause describes the cause and the 'result' clause describes the effect.

There are different kinds of conditional sentences. In zero conditional sentences, we use the present simple in both clauses. We use **if** to link the clauses.

Condition	Result
You press that button.	The door opens.

If + present simple   present simple
If you press that button, **the door opens.**

The result clause can come before the condition clause. We only use a comma (,) when the **if** clause comes first.

Result	Condition
The door opens if you press that button.	

* **1** ▶ **26.1** Match 1–6 with a–g. Listen and check, then listen and repeat.

  ▶ If you don't eat healthy food, _g_
  1 If you don't eat, ___
  2 If you don't drink, ___
  3 If you don't sleep, ___
  4 If you stay too long in the sun, ___
  5 If you spend too much time alone, ___
  6 If you don't do any exercise, ___

  a you get hungry.
  b you get unfit.
  c you get sunburn.
  d you get thirsty.
  e you get lonely.
  f you get tired.
  g ~~you get ill.~~

* **2** ▶ **26.2** Listen and number the pictures.

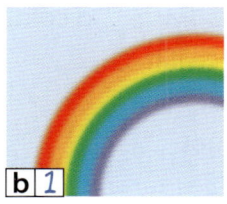

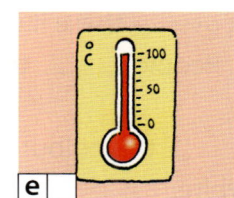

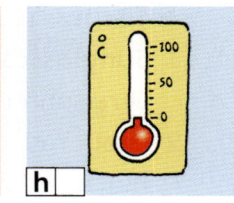

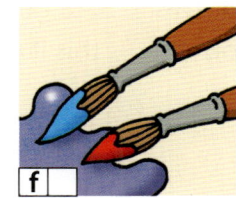

Unit 26 145

3 ▶ 26.3 Complete the sentences with the correct form of the verbs in brackets. Then listen again and check.

1 **A rainbow** If it _'s_ (be) sunny and raining at the same time, this _appears_ (appear) in the sky.
2 **100°C** If you _____ (heat) water to this temperature, it _____ (boil).
3 **Venus flytrap** This plant _____ (close) if an insect or spider _____ (walk) on it.
4 **Purple** You _____ (get) this colour if you _____ (mix) red and blue.
5 **Brown** You _____ (see) this if you _____ (mix) all the colours of the rainbow together.
6 **Cacti** These plants _____ (be) OK if they _____ (not get) much water.
7 **100°C** Water _____ (freeze) if it _____ (cool) to this temperature.
8 **Icicles** These _____ (form) if water _____ (drip) and _____ (freeze).

4 ▶ 26.4 Complete the zero conditional definitions with the verbs in the correct form. Listen and check.

be cut get ~~have~~ keep
mix need rain ~~use~~ wear

▶ **Tissues** You _use_ these if you _have_ a cold.
1 **Sunglasses** People _____ these if it _____ very sunny.
2 **Grey** You _____ this colour if you _____ black and white.
3 **An umbrella** This _____ you dry if it _____.
4 **A plaster** You _____ this if you _____ your finger.

5 GAME Cover the sentences in exercise 4. Look at the pictures. How many definitions can you remember?

6 How well do you know your partner? Guess, and circle, your partner's answers. Then talk to your partner to see if you are right ✓ or wrong ✗.

You …	✓ / ✗
cry / don't cry if you watch a sad film.	
laugh / don't laugh if someone tickles your feet.	
get in a bad mood / feel fine if you don't have any breakfast.	
are **patient / impatient** if you have to wait for something for a long time.	
read / sleep / look out of the window / listen to music / start a conversation with a stranger if you go on a long train or bus journey.	
ask for help / don't ask for help if you can't do something.	
get angry / stay calm if someone gets cross with you.	
get anxious / feel happy if someone talks to you in English.	
say hello / smile / don't do or say anything if you see your neighbour.	
feel happy / anxious if someone gives you a baby to hold.	

You don't cry if you watch a sad film.

No, that's not true! I cry!

7 Write about your partner. Use the information from exercise 7.

Edward cries if he watches a sad film but he doesn't laugh if someone tickles his feet. He …

146 Zero conditional

8 Look at the picture and complete the sentences with the 'Action' and 'Result' verbs in the correct form.

Blow the whistle once for music.
Blow the whistle twice for the music to stop.
Turn the handle for chocolate.
Pull the lever for a back massage.
Push the lever for a head massage.
Ring the bell for a hot meal (a robot brings it).
Press the button for a glass of cold water.

Action
blow ~~blow~~ press
pull push turn ring

Result
get give get bring
massage ~~play~~ stop

▶ If you <u>blow</u> the whistle once, music <u>plays</u>.
1 If you _____ the whistle twice, the music _____.
2 If you _____ the lever, the machine _____ you a back massage.
3 If you _____ the lever, the machine _____ your head.
4 If you _____ the handle, you _____ chocolate.
5 If you _____ the bell, a robot _____ you a hot meal.
6 If you _____ the button, you _____ a glass of cold water.

9 Work in small groups. Design one of the machines below. What levers, buttons and handles does the machine have? What do they do? Write about the machine using zero conditional sentences.

The Hot Day Machine
The Snowy Day Machine
The 'I Can't Get to Sleep' Machine
The 'I Need to Get Fit' Machine

THE SNOWY DAY MACHINE
If you press this button, your clothes get warmer and ...

10 Explain your machine to other groups. Whose machine do you like the best?

This is our machine. It's called 'The Snowy Day Machine'. It's very clever. If you press this button, your clothes get warmer and if you ...

Self-evaluation Rate your progress.

	😊	😊😊	😊😊😊
1			
2			
3			
4			
5			
6			
7			
8			
9			
10			

Unit 26

Revision 8 Units 25–26

Reading and writing

1 Match 1–5 with a–h to complete the conversation. You don't need to use all the letters.

▶ 💬 It's nine o'clock.
💬 _b_

1 💬 I like this green paint – and I like this blue paint.
💬 ___

2 💬 OK. Anything else I need to know?
💬 ___

3 💬 What do you mean?
💬 ___

4 💬 OK, I'll be careful. Can we start now?
💬 ___

5 💬 Oh no! I'll go and get some.
💬 ___

a If you get this paint on your clothes, it doesn't wash out.
b ~~Yes, and we've got a lot to do, so we should start now.~~
c I think so … but we haven't got any brushes!
d We need this because the paint is very old.
e Yes. Don't get paint on your clothes because it'll ruin them.
f If you do that, the paint dries very quickly.
g OK. If you do that, I can put these newspapers down.
h The blue's lovely, but there isn't a lot of it, so don't use too much.

2 Read the article. Choose the right words below and write them on the lines.

Reading

Reading is an excellent way to improve your English. There are lots of stories for students of English, _so_ why not look for one in your school library ¹_____ bookshop today? Of course, there will be a lot of words that you don't understand, ²_____ you don't need to worry about every new word. It slows you down ³_____ you use a dictionary all the time. Keep reading, ⁴_____ you will find that some new words appear again ⁵_____ again. Make a note of these words ⁶_____ check them in a dictionary. You don't need to read different kinds of books in English. ⁷_____ you like reading crime stories in your own language, it's a good idea to read crime stories in English. Don't try to read books that are above your level ⁸_____ they will be too difficult ⁹_____ you won't be interested in them. Remember, you don't just have to read books. You can read newspapers ¹⁰_____ magazines in English too.

▶ (so) because but
1 or but so
2 if but because
3 because if or
4 so and if
5 or but and
6 and because so
7 If So Because
8 because so but
9 but and if
10 or but so

148 Units 25–26

Listening

3 ▶ R14.1 Listen and write.

VITAMINS AND MINERALS IN OUR DIET
▶ **A balanced diet** rice, pasta, meat, fish, cheese, nuts, _fruit_ and vegetables
1 **Vitamin** _____ keeps us healthy – found in tomatoes, potatoes and peppers
2 **Vitamin A** good for growth and our _____
3 **Vitamin** _____ important for strong muscles
4 **Vitamin D** good for our bones and _____
5 **Vitamin D** in fish and milk and from _____

4 ▶ R14.2 What do the buttons on the TV remote control do? Listen and write a letter (a–f) in each box.

a makes picture brighter
b switches TV on and off
c changes TV to DVD
d makes sound louder
e changes channel
f makes sound quieter

1 b
2
3
4
5
6

Speaking

5 Look at the pictures and tell the story.

6 Ask and answer the questions with a partner.

Do you prefer mornings or evenings? Why?

What do you do if you wake up very early in the morning?

What do you do if you feel tired and sleepy in the afternoon?

Do you prefer reading or listening to music at bedtime? Why?

What do you do if you can't get to sleep at night?

Do you prefer mornings or evenings?
I prefer mornings.
Why?
Because I …

Revision 8

Revision 9 All units

Reading and writing

1 Look and read. Choose the correct words and write them on the lines.

> apples balloons ~~carrots~~ feathers future
> iron history potatoes present roof sky

▶ They're orange. They grow under the ground. _carrots_

1 It's already happened. It can't happen again. _____
2 You have to cook them if you want to eat them. _____
3 It hasn't happened yet. _____
4 It's above us. We can see it but we can't touch it. _____
5 It's happening now. _____
6 It's made of metal. It makes clothes flat and it makes them look smart. _____
7 They're light. You might find them on the ground. Birds have them. _____
8 They're round. They're made of rubber. You fill them with air or gas. _____

3 Look at the picture and read. Write 'yes' or 'no'.

▶ The woman's eating. _no_
1 The grey cloud looks like a hand. _____
2 The man has already caught some fish. _____
3 There aren't any boats, cars or planes. _____
4 The baby is crying noisily. _____

2 Read the text and write the missing words. Write one word on each line.

> above below ~~ever~~ last lot
> many so when walked walking

The Kalka-Shimla Hill Railway
Have you _ever_ been on a really amazing train ride? I have. I went on the Kalka-Shimla Hill Railway ¹_____ I was visiting family in India with my parents ²_____ year. The train leaves Kalka station at 656 m ³_____ sea level. It climbs 1420 m to Shimla station, high up in the mountains. There are a ⁴_____ of tunnels and bridges on the way. One thing surprised me. We saw local people ⁵_____ on the railway track. That doesn't seem safe to me.

5 The tennis racket is against the picnic basket. _____
6 The ball is smaller than the picnic basket. _____
7 The boy in the red T-shirt is the youngest person in the picture. _____

150 All units

4 What does Amy say to Robert? Match 1–5 with a–h. You don't have to use all the letters.

▶ 💬 _b_
🗨 No, they're chocolate truffles.
1 💬 ___
🗨 I didn't buy them. I made them.
2 💬 ___
🗨 I mixed warm chocolate with cream.
3 💬 ___
🗨 Of course. Go ahead.
4 💬 ___
🗨 They're good, aren't they?
5 💬 ___

a How long do you have to cook them?
b ~~Are those chocolate cakes?~~
c That tastes delicious!
d How did you make them?
e Yes, they're better than chocolate cakes!
f May I have that little truffle?
g Do you like making cakes?
h Were they expensive?

5 Read the letter and write the missing words. Write one word on each line.

Dear Brian,

You've heard about my plans for a trip to the jungle, _haven't_ you? I'm ¹_____ to study some very unusual butterflies, and I think it'll be very interesting.

²_____ Suzy tell you about her adventures in the jungle last year? ³_____ had a lot of difficulties and got ill, too. ⁴_____ worry about me. I'll be fine. I've got a good guide and I've been to that jungle three times.

Now, I must go and pack my bags. I ⁵_____ even started packing!

Richard

6 Read the article. Choose the right words and write them on the lines.

Emperor Penguins

Where do Emperor Penguins live?
Emperor Penguins live _in_____ Antarctica, at the South Pole. ¹_____ spend the entire winter on the open ice. No other animals do this.

²_____ big are Emperor Penguins?
Emperor Penguins are about 115 cm high. They are the ³_____ kind of penguin in the world.

⁴_____ is the life cycle of Emperor Penguins?
⁵_____ winter the female Emperor Penguin lays one egg. She ⁶_____ the egg with the male, then goes away for two months to find food. A strong wind makes the temperature ⁷_____ to about -50°C, but under the male penguin's body the egg is nice and ⁸_____. Incredibly, the male penguin doesn't eat ⁹_____ food at this time. After two months the female returns ¹⁰_____ looks after the chick. The male goes away to find food.

▶ (in) on   at
1 It   He   They
2 What   How   Who
3 big   bigger   biggest
4 What   How   When
5 At   On   Every
6 leaves   's leaving   left
7 fall   falling   to fall
8 warmly   warm   warmest
9 any   some   many
10 so   and   because

Revision 9   **151**

Listening

7 ▶ R15.1 Listen and draw lines.

Jenny   Angie   Martin   George

Polly   William   Sally   John

8 ▶ R15.2 Listen and write.

NEW ART GALLERY
- ▶ When did it open? _last_ month
- 1 What kind of art? _____ art
- 2 Where is it? _____ the post office
- 3 Price _____ for Student Card holders
- 4 Closed _____
- 5 take photos – OK? _____

9 ▶ R15.3 What sports do the people in Anna's family do? Listen and write the sport.

- ▶ Anna's dad _running_
- 1 Anna's brother _____
- 2 Anna _____
- 3 Anna's sister _____
- 4 Anna's aunt _____
- 5 Anna's grandma _____

10 ▶ R15.4 Listen and tick ✓ the correct picture.

▶ Where have Isabel and her dad been?
a ☐   b ☐   c ✓

1 What did they buy?
a ☐   b ☐   c ☐

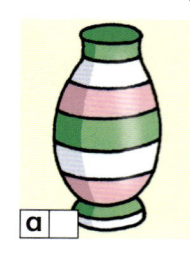

2 Where should Isabel put the box?
a ☐   b ☐   c ☐

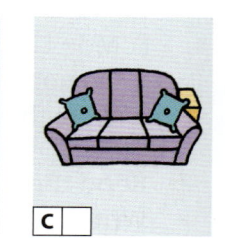

3 What will Isabel's dad use this afternoon?
a ☐   b ☐   c ☐

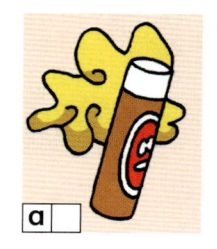

4 What's Isabel going to do before lunch?
a ☐   b ☐   c ☐

5 Which is Isabel's lunch?
a ☐   b ☐   c ☐

152   All units

Speaking

11 Work in pairs. Look at the pictures. Can you find 10 differences?

In Picture 1 there are two tables but in Picture 2 there are six tables.

Picture 1

Picture 2

12 Look at the pictures and tell the story.

The boy went to Europe's biggest music festival in 2010 and there were balloons with …

Revision 9 153

Extra information

Unit 3

Articles and quantifiers

9 **Look at the pictures on page 16 for two minutes, then answer the questions below.**

▶ How many jars of water are there? 6
1 How many pots of paint are there? ___
2 Are there six tubs of glitter? ___
3 How many tubes of glue are there? ___
4 How many pieces of paper are there? ___
5 Are there seven bags of clay? ___
6 How many bottles of ink are there? ___
7 Are there two rolls of brown paper? ___
8 How many sticks of charcoal are there? ___

Unit 10

Past continuous

9 **Look at the picture for two minutes, then answer the questions on page 55.**

Unit 13, student A

Imperatives

8 **Student B is at the station. Give him or her directions to these places.**

the café   the lake   the museum

1 It's a mystery tour, so don't tell student B where he or she is going. Use these phrases.

Go … / Don't go …   Turn left/right …
Take the first/second left/right …

2 Now you are at the station. Listen to student B's directions. Where does he or she take you?

Unit 24

Question tags

14 **The ten errors on page 136 are:**

1 Sunflowers are yellow or orange, not blue.
2 Camels have one or two humps, not three.
3 Oranges contain lots of vitamin C, not vitamin A.
4 $7 \times 7 = 49$.
5 Beef comes from cows, not sheep. Lamb comes from sheep.
6 The capital of Venezuela is Caracas, not Buenos Aires. Buenos Aires is the capital of Argentina.
7 H_2O is water, not carbon dioxide. Carbon dioxide is CO_2.
8 Butterflies don't make honey; bees do.
9 People first landed on the moon in the 1960s.
10 Spain won the football World Cup in 2010.

Unit 18, student A

Adjectives

14 Talk about the pictures with student B. Are they the same or different? Write S or D.

Picture 1 _D_

Picture 2 ___

Picture 3 ___

Picture 4 ___

Picture 5 ___

Picture 6 ___

Picture 7 ___

Picture 8 ___

Picture 1 is a picture of a small black dog.

The dog in my picture is small but it's white. That's different.

Unit 23, team B

Question words

16 General knowledge quiz. Play the quiz.

Team B

1 Prepare quiz questions from the information.
2 Answer questions from team A.
3 Ask team A your quiz questions.
4 The team with the most correct answers wins.

How old is the Eiffel Tower?

I think it's 160 years old.

No, it's 130 years old!

The Eiffel Tower
The Eiffel Tower is around 130 years old. It's 300 metres high.

1 100 / 130 / 160 years old?
   How old is the Eiffel Tower?
2 100 / 200 / 300 metres high?
   _____

Male peacock, tail feather
Male peacocks have around 200 tail feathers. Each tail feather is about 150 cm long.

3 200 / 300 / 400 tail feathers?
   _____
4 the tail feathers: 75 cm / 150 cm / 175 cm long?
   _____

The human brain
The human brain is a pinkish-brown colour. The average adult human brain weighs about 1.5 kilos.

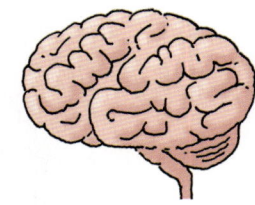

5 pinkish-brown / greyish-white / greyish-pink colour?
   _____
6 about 1 / 1.5 / 2 kilos?
   _____

Extra information 155

Unit 18, student B

Adjectives

14 Talk about the pictures with student A. Are they the same or different? Write S or D.

Picture 1 _D_

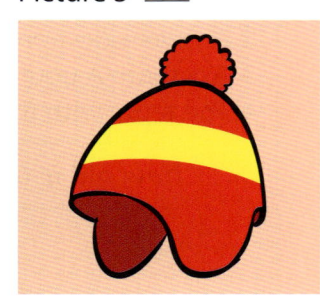

Picture 2 ___

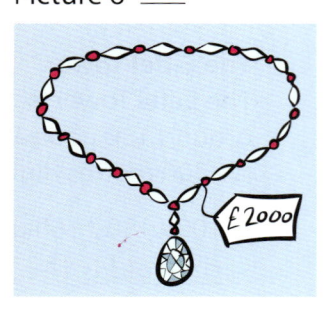

Picture 3 ___

Picture 4 ___

Picture 5 ___

Picture 6 ___

Picture 7 ___

Picture 8 ___

> Picture 1 is a picture of a small black dog.

> The dog in my picture is small but it's white. That's different.

Revision 5, student B

Speaking

6 Work in pairs. Student B look at the information below. Student A turn to page 114. Complete the table. Ask your partner questions to get the information you need. Use the prompts.

The smallest bird in the world

Name	The Bee Hummingbird
Bigger than a bee?	
Bigger than a large spider?	
Colour	
Male bird or female bird bigger?	
How often / male sit on the eggs?	

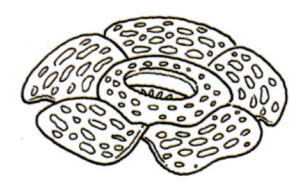

The biggest flower in the world

Name	The Rafflesia
Heavier than a one-year-old child?	yes
Bigger than a large bicycle wheel?	yes
Colour	red, brown and white
Smell	horrible
How often / it / produce a flower?	hardly ever

> What's the smallest bird in the world?

> The Bee Hummingbird.

> What's the biggest flower in the world?

> The Rafflesia.

156 Extra information

Revision 7, student B

Speaking

6 Work in pairs. Student A look at the information below and student B turn to page 138. Complete the table. Ask your partner questions to get the information you need. Use the prompts.

Bus to city centre

bus stop / it leave from	
long / the journey	
much / a single ticket cost	
often / the bus	
time / next bus	
where / buy a ticket?	

Train to city centre

platform / it leave from	number 7
long / the journey	20 minutes
much / a single ticket cost	six pounds
often / the train	every 15 minutes
time / next train	2.30
where / buy a ticket?	at the ticket office

What bus stop does the bus to the city centre leave from?

Number nine.

What platform does the train to the city centre leave from?

Number seven.

Unit 13, student B

Imperatives

10 Student A is at the station. Give him or her directions to these places.

the swimming pool   the tower   the beach shop

Go … / Don't go …   Turn left / right …
Take the first / second left / right …

Extra information 157

Word list

Word	Unit
a few	11, 12, 19, 22
a little (adj, det)	9, 12
after	22
ago	22
air	9, 25
already	19
angry	5, 7, 19, 26
anything	26
anywhere	13
arrive	11
artist	1
astronaut	6
aunt	20
away	10
bark (v)	7
before	22
begin	9
bin	13, 16, 21
blow (v)	8, 26
boat	3, 7, 8, 9
bored	7, 16
born	9, 11, 22, 23
bottom	12, 21
break (v)	11, 23
bridge	13
broken	11, 14
brush (n, v)	2, 11, 8, 19, 22
build (v)	11
burn (v)	11
bus stop	21
butter	3
butterfly	1
button	26
calm (adj)	5, 7, 26
camel	24
camp (v)	11
card	15
career	19
caterpillar	1
ceiling	12, 21
century	22
charcoal	3
chat (v)	6, 9, 11, 12, 22
cheap	18, 20
clay	16
club	8, 23, 24
colourful	18, 20
comfortable	7, 19, 20
comic	3
competition	6
cook (n)	8
cotton	5, 18
could (v)	14, 24
cross (v)	13
cry (v)	5, 8, 9, 10, 11, 23, 26
cut (v)	7, 11, 12, 26
dance (v)	5, 6, 9, 14, 19, 25
dangerous	12, 18, 20, 25
dark	10, 18, 21
date (n)	22
dear (adj)	6, 9, 12
decide	10, 12
dentist	6, 16, 22, 23
desert	11, 20, 25
diamond	20, 21
diary	8, 17
dictionary	1, 11, 13, 15, 19
dinosaur	18, 22
direction	13
dirty	8, 10, 18
donkey	2
drum (n)	10
dry	12, 17, 20, 25, 26
duck (n)	4, 10
east	13, 25
engineer	18
ever	11
everyone	5
everything	5, 9, 16, 18
exam	6, 9, 12, 17, 22, 23, 24, 25
excellent	23
factory	16
fall	5, 9, 10, 11, 12, 24
fall over	10
famous	6, 12, 18
far (adj, adv)	4, 12, 14
fast (adj, adv)	18, 19, 20, 23, 24
feel	7, 15, 16, 18, 19, 20, 26
finish (v)	8, 9, 11, 19, 22
fire (n)	12, 13, 14, 16
fix	11, 12, 14
flour	3
fly (n)	2
follow	13
forest	9, 21
forget (v)	11, 13
friendly	18, 20
front	21
full	24
fun (adj, n)	7, 12, 20
future	12, 15, 23
gate	13
get off	10
get on	10
get to	23, 26
glass (adj)	5, 7, 18, 21, 24, 25, 26
glitter	3
glove	2, 10
glue (n, v)	3
go out	6, 13, 25, 26
gold (adj, n)	3, 6, 20
golf	6, 19, 24
goose	2
ground (n)	6, 13, 21
group	9, 20, 25
grow	5, 11, 21
half (adj, n)	8, 10, 16, 22
happen	10, 11, 12
hard (adj, adv)	11, 16, 19
hardly	19
hate	6, 12
hear	4, 7, 14
heavy	18, 20
high	23
hill	21
hit (v)	9, 10
honey	3, 7, 18, 24
hotel	11
hour	9, 11, 22
husband	8, 19
ice (n)	3
icicle	26
ill	5, 10, 25, 26
important	11, 12, 16, 18, 23
ink	3
insect	20
interesting	4, 7, 18, 20
into	10, 11
invent (v)	6, 9, 12
jam (n)	3
job	6

word	pages
journalist	8
journey	9, 25
just	15
kilo	2, 3
kilometre	14
kind (adj)	17
knife	2
land (v)	10, 15
language	20
late (adj, adv)	6, 9, 13, 18, 19, 25
later	12, 25
laugh (v)	5, 7, 9, 10, 26
leather	5, 18
leave (v)	9, 11
left (adj, n)	13
lie down	9
light (adj, n)	13, 18
lightning	9
litre	3
litter (n)	13
little	12
look like	7, 18
lovely	24
made of	5, 24
magazine	3, 6, 20
married	11, 12
maths	12, 19, 25
may (v)	15
meal	18, 24
medicine	5, 12, 16
meet	8, 9, 19, 21
metal (adj, n)	5, 18
midnight	22
might	15
minute	11, 22
mix (v)	26
modern	18
month	11, 20, 22
moon	1, 6
much (adv, det, pron)	3, 4, 16, 23
museum	14, 16, 18
necklace	3, 2, 20
news	19
newspaper	8, 21
next (adj, adv)	21, 22
noisy	9, 19, 20
north	13
of course	14, 15, 24
office	20
once	11, 19
other (det, pron)	3, 21, 25
outside	6, 17, 25
over (adv, prep)	16
paint (n)	3, 10
paper (adj, n)	3, 5
past (n, prep)	9, 23
pepper	5
photographer	8
piece (n)	3
pilot	6, 8, 24
pizza	6, 18, 23, 25
planet	9
plastic (adj, n)	5, 7
player	7, 9, 20, 23
pocket	9, 21
policeman/woman	7
pollution	3, 5
pony	2
post (v)	4, 12
post office	20
postcard	12
prefer	25
press (v)	26
problem	9
programme	24
pull (v)	26
push (v)	26
quarter	22
queen	1
radiator	21
rainbow	2, 15, 26
rarely	19
ready	18
recently	11
relaxed	5
remember	1
rich	6, 12, 20
right (adj, n)	13
ring (n, v)	2, 9, 18, 26
rubber (material)	5
rubbish (n)	3, 16, 21
rug	21
safe	18, 20
salt (n)	3
same	22, 23, 24
scissors	3
scream (v)	5
seatbelt	1
secret	12
seem	7, 18
sell	4
send	12
shelf	2, 12, 17, 20
should	17
silver (adj, n)	3, 24
since	11
sing (v)	5, 6, 7, 8, 9, 10, 16
singer	8, 20
ski (n, v)	6, 12, 19, 22, 24, 25
sky	1, 12, 26
slice (n)	3
smell (n, v)	7, 14, 18, 19
sneeze (v)	5, 12
snow (n)	5
snowman	7
so (adv, conj)	17, 25
soap	3
someone	7, 15, 23, 26
soon	8, 12
sound (n, v)	7, 18, 19
south	13
space	21
speak	6, 8, 13, 19, 24
spend (v)	9, 16
spicy	5, 25
spin (v)	5
spoon	3
spoonful	3
stamp (n)	1, 23
station	13, 21
stay	6, 9, 11, 24, 26
steal	12
still (adv)	19
storm (n)	9
straight ahead	13
straight on	13
strange	18
strong	5, 20
study (v)	8, 9, 11, 16, 23
suddenly	10
sugar	3
suitcase	25
sure	12
surname	24
sweet(s)	5, 14, 17
taste (n, v)	7, 18, 19
taxi	17, 25
teach	16
team	20
teenager	19
tent	8, 9
thank (v)	6, 16, 25
theatre	21

Word list **159**

Word	Unit
thirsty	5, 6, 19, 26
through	9, 23
tidy (adj, v)	6, 9, 16, 22
tin	3
together	19
tomorrow (adv, n)	8, 12, 22
tonight (adv, n)	12, 23
traffic	3
trophy	6
tube	3
turn (v)	13
twice	11, 19
uniform (n)	16
university	21
until	11
use (v)	11, 13, 15, 26
usually	9, 19, 22
warm	1, 7, 9, 21, 25
way	2, 25
west	13
where	9, 10, 20, 21, 23
whistle (v)	7, 26
wife	2, 19
will (v)	12, 18, 23, 24
win (v)	6, 9, 11, 12, 22, 24
wish (n)	6
wolf	2, 20
wood	5, 20
wool	5
year	2, 8, 22
yet	19
zero	26

Irregular verb list

Base form	Past simple	Past participle
be	was	been
become	became	become
begin	began	begun
break	broke	broken
bring	brought	brought
build	built	built
buy	bought	bought
catch	caught	caught
come	came	come
cost	cost	cost
do	did	done
drink	drank	drunk
drive	drove	driven
eat	ate	eaten
fall	fell	fallen
feel	felt	felt
find	found	found
fly	flew	flown
forget	forgot	forgotten
get	got	got
give	gave	given
go	went	gone, been
have	had	had
hear	heard	heard
know	knew	known
leave	left	left

Base form	Past simple	Past participle
lose	lost	lost
make	made	made
meet	met	met
pay	paid	paid
put	put	put
read	read	read
run	ran	run
say	said	said
see	saw	seen
send	sent	sent
sing	sang	sung
sit	sat	sat
sleep	slept	slept
speak	spoke	spoken
spend	spent	spent
stand	stood	stood
swim	swam	swum
teach	taught	taught
take	took	taken
tell	told	told
think	thought	thought
understand	understood	understood
wake	woke	woken
wear	wore	worn
win	won	won
write	wrote	written